# Journey Of The Heart...

## Written by

## Cathy L. Kaiser

ISBN: 1-40330-975-2

This book is printed on acid free paper.

1stBooks - rev. 05/23/02

# Table of Contents

# I Choose To Dance!

A song leaps from my heart at the
beginning of each new day,
A song with a melody that
never plays a sad song,
never carries a tune that is wrong,
this is just my way…
If I have choice of sitting this one out,
I will choose to dance!

If there is breath of life
there is always hope of life,
love and great things to experience and know!
It is so important if there is
love of the heart, to let it show!

Some live a life that never know real sorrow,
some face sorrow more
than it seems they should.
Some we say, have more than their share,
but still face it as much as they could.
If you have a choice dance, dance, dance!

Even in the face of sorrow,
I don't want to sit this one out,
Even in the face of tears, I don't want to sit this one out, I want to
choose to dance!
I hope with all my heart, that no matter come what may, that you will
always choose to dance! Dance of the heart, dance of the soul,
dance with all your might,
dance with courage, never letting go.
Choose To Dance!

# I KNEW A MAN...

**I knew a man...**
That answered all my questions never raising his voice—
Always had a kind word for all he knew—this was his choice!

**I knew a man...**
That graciously gave his never ending hugs, and gentle smiles,
and his heart always big enough to reach across the miles.

**I knew a man...**
With strong, not slothful, but caring hands, for this he would do,
and because of his love for God, yes he even loved you!!

**I knew a man...**
Always lending his heart and embrace, with his bright blue eyes full
of grace.

**I knew a man...**
Whose words of comfort, his hearty laughter made me feel the best,
his love took care of all the rest.

**I knew a man...**
That went home to Jesus and
I loved him so,
yes it was time for him to go.

**I knew a man...**
I shall continue to endlessly love, and cherish all that we have today,
and I will miss him—this I must say, you may ask me this one
question
before I am done, Who was this man?!? This man was grandpa, one
of God's sons.

## I knew a man...

That will keep watching over me,
each and everyday,
for I can feel his love like a blanket assuring me all is okay.

## I Love You Grandpa!!

# The Ocean of Heart

As I stood and saw her grace
reached across the miles,
Tears trickled down my face
and left me with a smile.
I knew my heart belonged to her,
no one else could have it now,
for only her could embrace my soul and leave such a kiss of mist
upon my brow.
I could feel my spirit leave me and brush her gently with so much
love,
I felt I was touching her lightly, liken to a dove.
She made me feel so free, not a
problem as far as I could see.
She makes life seem so wonderful,
just simply to be.

As I walked arm in arm with my love on that wondrous beach,
I felt as if all my desires and hopes for the first time were just within
my reach.
I will return to her over and over and over again this you must know
for a fact,
I will always welcome her powerful presence and feel in her is
nothing lack.
Her grace whispers with rushing sounds,
her beauty causes your very soul to abound.
Her power overwhelms every heart, that lays their eyes upon her
grace,
she whispers with such love,
and spreads wonderful
mist of freshness upon your face.

Her waves of great power takes you so completely that you never
want to leave.
And holds you so tight that you feel at peace, no place inside of you is
left to grief.

4

Standing in her presence, getting close to her—is all you want to do.
And all you can think about is her
and about you.
She is so sensuous, so graceful,
so filled with heart,
it saddens you when night fall comes and you must finally part.
From the first moment you lay
your eyes upon her beauty,
you are speechless and appreciate her fully, for you know it is your
duty.

This is how I felt as I viewed her, the Pacific Ocean, for the very first
time, today.
I will never see things quite the same again, at least not in the very
same way.

When my body grows old and tired
and I give myself to death,
drawing that very last breath,
I will spring to new life and feel no more pain,
And feel only good things as my loved ones blend my ashes there,
I will be rushing in one of her waves, plus maybe in the gentle rain.
This with you is what my heart
desires to share.

In all her gentle sounds I will whisper of all her
wondrous love, I will be with her forever and far as the eyes can see,
for I only know that this is destiny
and destiny must just be.

*Cathy L. Kaiser*

# AN INNOCENT CHILD WAS BORN...

**On a December day, an innocent child
was born,**

To give all of the world love and hope,
To give each in our hearts such peace that passes all understanding.
This alone would help us to daily cope.

**On a December day an innocent
child was born,**

To give the world a dream,
To give the world a vision,
To give the world a chance,
To give the world what it truly
needs or so it seems,
even if you only take a glance.

**On a December day an innocent
child was born,**

born in the darkest of nights,
a light for all to see!
To give all an opportunity
to make their lives full
of joy and happiness just could be,
To make this possible this child
died upon a tree,
and rose again on day three.

**On a December day an innocent
child was born,**

This child grew to be a man and did just what had to be done,
Now we can choose
through His love to be free!

**This child that was born
on a December day,**

Who is this child you may ask me,
who could it be?
The answer is simple, this little child was God's very own son.
Through Him all things are possible,
but only through Him,
the door can only be opened by Him,
for He is the key.

**Who is this child, what is his name?**

A name uttered by so many.
A named claimed by so much joy.
A named prayed so often.
His name is Jesus Christ, the Savior for all.
Jesus, who loves us gives us
completeness of heart.
A Savior that is merely waiting for your call.

# I'LL BE THERE

When you have the most of
hard times in your life
and do not know where to turn or where it might be bound,
When your life is in such turmoil there are no answers to be found,

## I'll be there

When the sun hits your face
and warms it to your delight,
when you accomplish the
most difficult of all tasks
and you jump for joy with all your might.

## I'll be there

When you have the most happiest
days of your life
and need someone to share of its splendor,
when you have all you want and are busting with happiness and joy,
and just need to share about its sender.

## I'll be there

When things around you are
rushing in like waves and
you do not know where to turn,
When life seems to have given
you a rough ride and you
don't know what to do, but you
just feel as if you might burn.

## I'll be there

I'll always be there to hold your hand,
and hold you in the hardest
and darkest of times,
I'll always be there to celebrate
when things are the
most content and it all makes you feel sublime.
When it all makes you
feel like jumping for joy with
a dance, when at last you feel life has given you that one chance.

## I'll be there

I'll always be there in good times and bad, I'll be there to make sure
you know just how much your friendship is treasured as gold.
If you will allow me to say this, to be so bold.

## I'll be there

I'll be there to encourage you
go on just one more mile,
to push you to do more to do better,
and to do it with a smile!
To be your cheering section when you accomplish your best
And my dearest friend,
I think you know the rest.

## I'll always be there.

# CHOICES

Pain is the darkest of things
that could possibly come,
It tries to steal your joy, and kills your soul when it thinks it is done.
But it cannot steal your inner self, that is up to you to decide its task.
It is in reality merely a mask.
Pain can take your joys
and parade them as sorrow,
pain can destroy all you
spent your whole life doing,
it is a choice you make
or perhaps only to borrow.
Yes just a choice, so choose the positive choice that is what you need
to do
Pain can give you heartache and grief,
or you can choose to only let it get you down—all so brief.

Pain can be a killer there is no doubt,
but if you hang on to all the joys you have, and because of them give
a shout.
It will set you free from all the pain, at least for a very short time,
It can give you relief in your very own mind.
Pain comes in so many different forms
not just the body or the heart can it swarm.
You decide on what you focus on the most,
you decide inside of you
that you wish to boast.
For if you let it capture you a little bit too long,
It will introduce you to its partner, depression, that sings a sad song.
My physical pain is only one
small part of who I am today,
It will not be my entire
focus or my total dismay.
No sir-ee I will live on and
make my life what I want it to be,
this is a merely choice, don't all of you see?

So make your choice solid each and every day
for it will determine your life happy or sad, it will choose your life
path and way.

# Living in Arizona

I sit and gaze at all God's creations from an Arizona Mountain,
It is amazing how he carved each one in it's separate delight.
They are so very breath taking from darkness to the first morning's
light.

It always astonishes me how
beautiful the sunsets are!
It overwhelms my soul,
as I look as I drive by in my car.

How the sun appears to set right on the mountain's tip at the end of
each day
How they seem to speak to you,
with their beauty and grace,
as you give yourself to their way.
How they take your breath
away with each part of its charm,
And you then realize that
here nothing will cause you harm.

You become so delighted in January,
to be in this state,
As you sit here and gaze at all of the beauty taking the hand of your
mate.
One day's drive you can be at the ocean, with all of its might,
and be amazed at the end of the day watching the darkness over the
ocean overwhelm the evening's light.
So having the privilege of living in such warmth, beautiful desert for
miles,
is more than a blessing
and brings more than one smile.

Then the summer comes
and takes you with a whirl,
the heat is so powerful your
head spins with a twirl.

You try to remember why
again do I love living here?
then you realize it is the weather
minus the summer
but through the summer the
memories will keep me near

Even though the summers
are a great big bummer.
The fall will come quickly and give me a break.
And then I will know, why again I love living here, for my own sake.

But where else can I live with nine months with the weather so nice?
no snow to shovel away, not one flake to worry
about I can say that thrice.

So for all that I love and
hold very dear to my heart,
while you are shoveling snow,
I am far from you apart,

Living where the weather is oh so very nice.
Sending your warm thoughts every single day.
So you can feel some of Arizona's weather coming your way!

# Our Journey Of Life...

Walking down the narrow journey road that comes by living every
day,
It is a rough road in places, some very smooth,
some very wide, some very narrow.

It looks as if this journey was planned out
centuries before my appearance on earth.
Sometimes the road so thin
that nothing can get
through almost except for a sparrow.
A journey known above,
yes before my very birth.

Do you wish to travel the road with me that is laid before me?
Do you wish to experience every pain, every joy that it will bring as I
walk?
Do you understand that the things that lie ahead are simply things that
should be?

We all treasure the joys that life so happily bestows on us as a gift.
We keep them close to our hearts and rejoice in them so freely,
and so many times that is our heart's truest lift.

But why aren't we as happy
in the face of pain?
The thing that molds us the most, the thing that shapes us to who
we are and are proud to be, that thing that makes me, me.
Is it so hard to see how very much through it we at times can possibly
gain?
Is it so difficult for all the
pain to really helps us see?

Is it so difficult to ponder
that in the face of diversities
that is shapes are very being,
It is not difficult for me to look beyond, it is not hard beyond the
surface seeing?

What would our character be like if all we experienced was the good?
What would our compassion be like, how would we feel all as we
should?

Look at hard times and pain
in body or soul as a gift from above,
Look at it as shaping us
from in detail with so much love.
Without it we would be lost in a twirling world
of not knowing what is good or bad,
We just wouldn't know if
we were happy or sad.

So look deep for the message I am trying so much to offer you here,
Look under the surface and for you allow my message to be very
clear.
For you with love and so very much care I am just only trying to say,
I want you to have all you can for your journey you walk on this very
day.

# Crossroads Of Life

The crossroads are before you,
which path will you take?
It is your choice, the right or the left,
it might make a difference
in the direction you choose to make.
It might be a small choice or one much larger on life's eventful scale,
what we choose or how we perceive things will give us the truest tale.

When things for us get oh so hard,
Do we choose to be negative
on the flip of a card?
Do we choose to be positive
and as happy as we can be?
Do we choose to laugh at diversities and just try the best to simply be
me?
Do we remain uplifting and
upbeat even if it is a lie,
Do we continue to be outgoing and happy, or do we change
and become somewhat shy?

Do we live to be honest and let the sorrow in?
Do we try to go on and grab
all the delight of life, or at
least once more try to begin?
What should we do, when life becomes filled with sorrow or grief,
What should we do when some are here with us on earth just all so
brief?
What do we do when the
tears flow as an ocean?
What do we do, when in our hearts there is no feeling nor motion?
What can we do when time
after time we are denied?
What can we do when no
more of happiness we are supplied?

Where are the joys we at
one time in our lives had?
Where are the joys, and when they left all we felt is oh so very sad.
How dark the hole can be
without even a glimmer of light
appears sometimes oh so very quick,

How that darkness
covers my soul so intensely,
that my very depths of my
soul starts to feel sick.
How it seems to be ready to
consume all I ever had known.
Where are the happiness
seeds I so carefully had sown?
Where are all the friends
I had been faithfully there for?

Where is the eagle with
spirit he used to for me soar?
Where is all the laughter
I used to hear and feel so deep within?
Where are the little things with hope I knew was just around the
bend?
Where are all my beliefs
that stood so very firm,
Just who am I, I wonder as
I look carefully in my reflection,
I was one that never could be beat, not me! Nothing could do me in!

Who is this I gaze upon in the mirror on this cool, darkest of nights,
who is this that looks so tired, so worn down, and filled with so much
dismay?
Who is this, that appears so dim, when I once was filled with so much
starlight?

17

Who is this, that looks
so weary of the journey that
has been painfully walked each day?
Where is the sparkle that my blue eyes once held so much of my soul?
Where is that hope that burst into a glow around all of me
with so much light and it
would to everyone really show?
What happened to all the things I set out to do, each and every goal?
And why is it now all left
more dark than the darkest coal?

So here I am at the crossroads one more time,
What will be my choice this
time I ask myself, quietly,
what choice will indeed be truly mine?
My head lowers as the options become more clear as I sit in the dark,
I lift my face up, and know what must be done
with not much time to pass,
I realized all along how I was
in this life and all I really
wanted was to do is make my special mark.
I knew what was important
what was the number one task,
and how I have becoming weary of wearing such a happy mask.

I believed in those happy statements and all of the thoughts I shared,
but what can I do now,
and how do I with this really bare?
How can I continue with
such sorrow in my heart?
How do I stay close to all I love, how do I honestly from this world
not part?
What are the answers or
crossroads I see before my eyes,
How do I find all or some of the
answers and stay positive
like I should and yet never utter,
no not one little lie?

So if you ever prayed or
cheered in my corner to help
my choices to be true or right,
This would be the crossroads that I sure could use a tad more light.

For death is not among my
many fears, but who I leave behind,
and I would weep as
their eyes filled with tears.
I could never hurt the ones
I treasure, I could never
make a choice that was selfish or was not kind.
I don't wish to make the wrong choices or to take the wrong road.

So I guess I am asking, that perhaps by prayer or a good thought for
me
you can lighten my load.

# True Friendships

Many think they truly know
what friendship means to all,
What all a friend should be,
or how to make the call.
How to be a friend in all senses of the word,
How to really be there, and keep the promises
breaking them are so painful but the pain many times are just
obscured.
But yet have no idea of what
hurt they have bestowed,
when each promise or word is broken,
and indeed it can make the
heart feel so ever low.

How they abandon in
the slight of a selfish moment.
How to break apart and know how to be a friend and what each thing
should be,
yes, each and every component.
Promises are so easy to make,
the words just flow right out,
saying I love you, is easy to say, harder to live, that is without a
doubt.

How do you live with the
broken promises you make?
How does your behavior reflect your promises, for goodness sake?
Can people truly sing praises how you never break your word
and you're always true?
Or do people when they think of your promises, just really feel sad
and blue?
How important is friendship to you, in the hour of your own needs?
How your friendships are merely the planting of your own seeds.

If you say "I love you," is the response
yes that I do know?
Or is it doubtful, and hard to believe,
and you are believed as
just putting on a show?
How is your friendship treasured
each and every day,
Is merely what you put into it,
and it makes its own way.

So if you look around and realize if there are not many you can really
trust,
perhaps you ought to take another look yourself in the mirror
yes sometimes this is a must.

For self improvement is a never ending thing,
It is something that we should
cherish and look at it and sing.

For if you are one that is deeply good inside,
You will always want to improve yourself so that true love can really
abide.

I speak with love and with the kindest of heart,
That I will always keep my word, and never from you part.

So if you feel as the world
is crashing on you hard,
Know there is a friend that is solid, and always will be the ace of all
the cards.
For I have never broken a promise or gone back on my word to this
very day,
And will always be here is what
I really came to say.

*Cathy L. Kaiser*

When I say "I love you" you can know the worlds are always true,
when I reach my hand out, you can count on it, of course this to you is
not new.

So let me offer you this one more thought,
That friendships take work, so they don't wear out and get shot.
They need love and attention to grow as anything does,
So they don't die and wither, that would be so sorrowful, just because.

# Just Being Me...

Sitting under the bright gleaming stars that shine through the night,
Knowing that my life is just a small part of the universe that is a dim
light.
But even still hoping it makes a difference to many, many lives before
I go.
To offer my heart, my love, and my life, that it might change just one
person to live positive, love life and let themselves glow.
To share my laughter, joys, and yes my sorrow and sadness,
To share it all, so I am complete and in perfect gladness.
To be a whole is to experience it all,
to find a good balance before that final call.
To know all things work out in their seasons,
To know they all have their special reasons.

Then the day comes when
from this earth I must go,
to finally have the full picture,
of things while here
I could not possibly know.
And then to become perfect
energy that never does die
From up above, shining for you to see,
in the darkest of night, this is no lie.
To be among the stars
gleaming finally so bright.
To reach a time when
all the sorrow makes sense,
To understand it all and why I was so tense.
To have learned every lesson that built my character as it should be,
To have experienced every thing, that made me—me.

Some so hard I didn't think I could get through,
Some with so many tears I didn't know
I was going to do.
Some with so much laughter and joy,
I thought I might burst.
Some with such grieving sorrow,
I wasn't sure what to do first.
But in through it all—
one thing always rings true,
That it carved myself into something special, so special that
many don't know, only a few.
So know this as you travel your way through all life's joys and trials,
That it's shaping something very special,
as your feet go the distance and the miles.

My grandpa always said to me: if hard times never came our way,
How would we really know
what was a good day?
How would we really know what to rejoice in?
How would we really know
what feels good then?
For there are so many lessons and answers that I really needed to find,
and for them all—I say thank you for teaching me so much
and giving me the path I should
take to learn these things,
and keeping my soul so kind.
So with this, I would like to say it is
difficult to add up how
many in your life, you touch.
But I hope that my life makes the
difference that it should,
I hope I have done all that I could.

# Do you know where your friends are?

Sometimes for reason unknown
sadness grips my very soul.
Sometimes for reasons untold, I fall short just before achieving my
goal.
Sometimes when I reach for
someone to be there,
I feel alone, so alone with no one to share.

Sometimes, in the dark of the night,
there is a hole through time,
I wish I could seep through it—It is like a music bar is to a chime.
Why does this sadness grip my
heart with so much strength?
Why does this darkness seem
to have so much length?
Why does it in my weakness
have so much delight?
. I know that it soaks up my inner light—and takes away my inner
sight.

Life is so full of surprises, black is white,
and white is black.
Who are your friends really?
Who are the ones that truly love you?
Who are the ones you think that love you,
but yet they lack?
It is a true surprise to find out in all of the realities who they really are.
When things come right down to it, your truest friends know what to
do.
And who they are, will surprise even you.

25

You thought Jack down the street,
was just a social guy every once in a while.
But when it came down to needing
the truest of friends,
he was the one at your door you first did meet.
He may was not that social,
and only came once and again,
but when you really needed him,
he was in a flash right there.
He was there, for you with arms
open only traveling one mile.
Yes he was there, showing
how very much he cared.

So be careful when you name your friends,
put them in a tidy list,
for you may have it backwards,
and have totally really missed.
Do you know who your friends really are?

# Reaching For One Gleaming Star

Reaching from the sky from a
chair bound with wheels,
having more love but a prisoner
in that chair even still.
How can I show all the love I have in my heart?
How can I feel whole this way,
how can I not fall apart?
How I want to reach just one gleaming star,
to reach for the dreams and hopes, oh but they seem indeed so very
far.

I used to rush around getting ready for the day,
simple things really, bathing,
dressing to simply say.
Until I viewed things from this
chair bound with wheels,
I never knew to be thankful for all those things I never gave thought
to,
Now, yes, now it is so very real.
It is not so easy to run my own bath,
and get in and out alone,
It isn't so easy to dress myself, as I once had.
To know each day that I need
help with these things,
only makes me incredibly sad.
Each day the illness takes me a
little more as it goes along,
each day it takes a piece of my heart, and I begin to sing a sad song.

Each day takes a part of my fighting spirit, I once had "I can beat anything"
Now I feel tired and just want to say it's done.
I want to just give up and say to my physical body, okay, okay you won.
How can I fight the pain everyday without wearing out,
How can I stay confident without any doubts?
My body is just weary, as the pain grows each day,
my body and spirit are tired, I guess that is what I needed to say.
I feel lost in the nothingness of space of pain, the joys and laughter I once had,
It just seems to me to be little sunshine, and mostly all rain.
I gaze at the stars thinking just a little more and I could reach a gleaming star,
Just reach a little higher, why it isn't really that far.
But my chair just sits way too low under the bursting lights above,
so I close my eyes and ask God to help me with all his mighty love.
So it is up to Him now to help or embrace me to come home.
I am counting on Him, to at the very least not let me do this alone.

# Life Happens

The sun sets, the sun rises
The heavens give rain, the sun shines bright
The night falls, the day gives its light
The moon covers its light over the earth,
A woman through pain gives to a child birth.
A promise given, a promise broken
A sickness happens, a death takes away.
Sadness such sadness that
life does freely give
Happiness such joy at times we can truly live.
Sorrow, true sorrow is the present it speaks,
It offers such pain to be pressed
against your very cheeks.
And just when the darkness falls
over the heart of man,
Just when he thinks he had
done just all he can.
He is given a glimmer of hope
that helps him push on.
It almost wears the clothing of the perfect con.
Lessons learned, lessons failed
Lessons of victory, lessons of defeat
Lesson we learn when we compete

So what can we say
about this thing called life?
Well for one thing we know it can be frustrating and have much strife.
But as always there is a glimmer of happiness, a glimmer of hope.
For look behind you and there is always a friend, one who loves you
that will help you cope.
Seize the day and make it all you can,
this is the key!

*Cathy L. Kaiser*

Make your own happy thoughts
and be all you can be
For it is the only way to live
to the fullest don't you see?

Sad times, happy times,
Times filled with sorrow,
times filled with ecstasy
Times filled with darkness,
times filled with gleaming light
Life is about how you receive,
how you react to all it gives to you,
So take it as it comes or don't, do what you feel you must do.
Take action, seize today, don't roll over, take your willful power
Use your strength, never run out of hope,
Always find a way to cope,
be true to yourself at all cost
And most of all believe in **YOU**

So each morning as you yawn
and stretch and meet the day,
Realize no matter what happens, Know for certain, it is you that has
the power!
The power to make your own way!!

# The Night is dark and long

I sit alone in the night as the
hours slowly creep by.
Sleep doesn't come at all, only in the depths of my heart is there a
desperate cry.
What realities can I not bear to face?
What in my heart that I
can find even one place?
What can I do, to calm such depth of sorrow,
What can I do so that I can face
each and every morrow?
Where is the strength I thought
I once possessed?
It feels so empty that I must to you confess.
How I use to be a tower of strength
and feel its arm embrace.
Within my whole inner essence,
Now I can't even feel even a
glimpse of it's presence.

I stretch out so far to reach
just one gleaming star of hope,
Oh but this prison chair of wheels,
it's seems so far, which
Makes it more difficult to cope.
The pain, the physical pain takes my soul and binds it up so very
tight,
It takes all I have to make it through the day, yes it takes away all my
might.
The laughter left and the pain appeared,
The pain goes through me liken to a spear.
Just when I thought all
hope was gone for good,
A glimmer of a bright star appears and tells me I can do it, and I really
should.

31

So I push on just one more day,
I realize no one really knows
what comes my way.
I smile just as nothing had ever
happened to bring me down,
I smile to prevent living with a frown.
So count each blessing life throws your way,
For it does come in handy when you are down and filled with dismay.
For there are good things somewhere in the midst of all the sadness,
There somewhere in that pile,
is at least a little gladness.

# Our Greatest Teacher

Pain, suffering, tears of sorrow,
happiness, laughter,
and sparkling eyes brighter than the sun,
accepting each part and
extending a hand so we
with each experience do not shun.
All part of living from day to day, month to month, year after year,
a journey of life taking it as it comes and sharing each tear.
Some facing more pains,
the whys we do not understand,
some facing more loss, still we do not understand the reasons.
All we know that God in his infinite wisdom can
turn each thing around for good—in his own season.

Holding on and trusting with all our might—it all has a place,
holding and trusting that God himself will show us a way and let us
touch his face.
It feels like we are holding on at times,
just by a thread,
It feels just like one more heart break, and I surely would be dead.
The Night falls so very black, yes so very dark
just when all hope is lost, God brings an answer and makes his
distinct mark.

I face physical pain each and every day,
I know this will not change—
for me it will just be the way.
I have learned new strengths that
I never could have known,
If it hadn't been for that one teacher, pain, and the seed in my life it
sown.
So look up with a cheerful heart and understand this one thing,
your darkest problem just might be your greatest salvation
that sings a song that rings!

*Cathy L. Kaiser*

# Praise him with Thanksgiving

Shout for the joy of the Lord, All the earth,
Shout and praise Him for His birth.
Look up and be thankful that God's caring hands holds us so tenderly
Look up and be glad that His hands holds our hearts so carefully.
Shout for the joy of the Lord, All the earth,
Shout and praise Him for His birth.
God's love is more worthy than silver or gold,
His love surrounds us like a warm
blanket and is not cold.
His love means more to me than
all the world has to give,
He has given me the finest treasures and now I can truly live!

Shout for the joy of the Lord, All the earth,
Shout and praise him for His birth.
He has shown me to look past
my body to the soul,
He has given me true mirth and honest goals.
Because of Him can my
heart really sing a song,
A song that is for the rest of my life long.
Shout for the joy of the Lord, All the earth,
Shout and praise Him for his birth.
Hand in hand with the Savior each day I walk,
Hand in hand each day the Lord and I, talk,
No matter come what may,
He will always be by my side,
This I heard Him say,
shout for the joy of the Lord,
All the earth, shout and praise Him for His birth.

# We Stand Together

Our friendship is one that cannot
be broken down,
It is solid and true and without fail it
is oh so very sound.
We will stand united throughout my entire life,
Our unity cannot be broken even through strife.
True friendships does not fail, does not crack, does not break,
When you need me I am there,
and when I need you most,
you are there, just for my sake,
to lift your glass to me and toast.
We are together, birds of the same feather!
Yes, we are together, you and I,

I can hear the birds sing with a song that has a sweet chime.
We are together, an unbeatable team,
we are together fighting the
odds it sometimes seems.
Together, together we will always win!
No matter come what may just around the bend.

Honesty, word of honor,
promises never broken,
these are the things that make our friendship forever lasting.
These are the things that created our friendship's casting.
As long as we are true we always
know just what to do.
As long as you love me and I love you, together we can face any task,
together there are no need for any masks.

We are together, you and I, for all time,
we are together, you and I.
I can hear the birds sing with a song
that has a sweet chime.
We are together, and unbeatable team,
we are together fighting the odds
it sometimes seems.

Together, together we will always win!
No matter come what may just around the bend.
Laughter, tears, sorrow, happiness,
we feel it, we share it all,

I am here to always take your call!
Laughing with you, wiping your tears away,
feeling your sorrow, sharing your joys,

Feeling it all, sharing it completely
isn't that what friendship is all about?
To share it all without a doubt?
We are together, you and I, for all time,
We are together, you and I.
I can hear the birds sing with
a song that has a sweet chime.

We are together, and unbeatable team,
we are together fighting
the odds it sometimes seems.
Together, together we will always win!
No matter come what may just around the bend.

# The Heart Of Laughter

The sweet sound of laughter—Is likened to music to the core of the
Living soul of man.
Laughter chords strike sweeter,
than Bach's symphony #5.
All those who surround it—
It causes them to burst with energy and
Feel so happy and alive!!
The sweet sound of laughter—
Eyes full of sparkle—the heart
Glows so very bright, sweet sounds of cheer—
Roll forth with tremendous might!! Rosy cheeks and a slap on the
knee,
A gaze upon your face, changes you forever—don't you see?

This describes laughter quite well, all a story does it indeed tell.
But it also describes our very beloved brother,
For our precious, beloved brother is laughter.
Not the sound you see, but the very heart.
For all he met, he touched,
To all people that knew him,
he meant so very much.
He had riches untold—
His heart and laughter were worth much
More than silver or gold.
No complaining, no sadness,
no feeling of grief,
One smile from his eyes made bad things seem so very brief.
So the next time you hear a hearty laugh
Think of our beloved brother
With a big smile and know that his
Laughter are chords, sounds of the soul!!
Know that they are sung from his very heart!
He will always be present in our laughter and that he will never from
us really ever part!!

# Reach Out to Jesus

Reach Out, Reach Out to Jesus He is waiting to hold you close,
Reach Out, Reach Out to Jesus it is He that loves you most.
Reach out, Reach out to Jesus it is He that loves you most.
When your troubled heart feels heavy and to handle it, well it's just
too much,
Reach out your arms to
Jesus and His hand you will touch!
Let Him carry you through your
hard times of suffering and pain—
Let Him mend your heart, I promise you will not remain the same.

Reach Out, Reach Out to
Jesus He is waiting to hold you close,
Reach Out, Reach Out to Jesus
it is He that loves you most.
Reach Out, Reach Out to Jesus
it is He that loves you most.
Let Him direct you in what
path or direction to take,
He will fill you with joy,
a new heart for you He'll make!
So the next time you feel
your heart breaking and filled with grief,
Give yourself to Jesus and
trust that it will be brief!
Reach Out, Reach Out to Jesus He is waiting to hold you close,
Reach Out, Reach Out to Jesus it is He that loves you most.
Reach Out, Reach Out to Jesus it is He that loves you most.

Our stubborn natures causes us to do everything on their own,
we suddenly get overwhelmed from the seeds we have sown.
But our loving Lord and Master waits for us to come back home,
His arms are always open, when things are finally done!
Reach Out, Reach Out to Jesus He is waiting to hold you close,
Reach Out, Reach Out to Jesus it is He that loves you most.

Reach Out, Reach Out to Jesus it is He that loves you most.
Reach out to grab a bright, and wondrous gleaming star,
I promise you, Jesus is not from you—
all that far!
He will always be right by your side,
For inside of you, His love
truly always will abide!!

Reach Out, Reach Out to Jesus He is waiting to hold you close,
Reach Out, Reach Out to Jesus it is He that loves you most.
Reach Out, Reach Out to Jesus He is waiting to hold you close,
Reach Out, Reach Out to Jesus it is He that loves you most.

*Cathy L. Kaiser*

# Dance, Dance, Dance!

Each morning as I awaken, I realize that it is yet another chance
another chance to rejoice,
another chance to gain strength,
yet another chance to feel life's presence through a dance.

So dance my friend, dance with all your might!
Dance and give your heart God's
amazing love light!
Each morning we all have choices
that we make every day,
we all make a choice on how
we greet the morning light,

so greet that morning light with sparkling eyes,
with a cheerful heart,
and with light and cheery soul,
greet it with all your might!
Choose my friend to dance!

So dance my friend, dance with all your might!
Dance and give your heart God's
amazing love light!

We all experience so many things,
sorrow, such sorrow,
happiness such gleeful happiness, sad times, painful times,
happy times, joyous times, times of laughter, times of flooding tears,
They all run into one other and mold us, create us, they make us,
yes create the real you, the only you.
So dance my friend, dance with all your might!
Dance and give your heart
God's amazing love light!
For how can we know how
joy feels without sadness?
How can we know how happiness

feels without sorrow?
How can we really look forward to the morrow?
In all things, learn to dance,
learn to feel grateful
to who we have become as a whole!
Learn to dance from your very soul!
So dance my friend, dance with all your might!
Dance and give your heart
God's amazing love light!

For when you feel that life is just not fair! That is time to dance if you
dare!
Then you will be amazed of what joy will leap into your very heart!
You will marvel at the happiness deep inside of you that cannot part!
For when you dance in the hardest of times, there is a peace that
passes all understanding that will give your soul the perfect chime.
So dance my friend, dance with all your might!
Dance and give your heart
God's amazing love light!

*Cathy L. Kaiser*

# Love Has No End

Such a simple word, with so few letters, what does the word **LOVE**
really mean?
The meaning changes with each person, each situation, each time and
place,
It can be more than one thing,
and is the simplest,
yet the most complicated
word in the human race.

**What is love?**

A touch of the hand?
A caress on a silky, soft cheek?
Fingers gently brushing through one's hair?
A slow, lingering, soft kiss upon one's lips?
A smile with sparkling loving eyes that shows how much one cares?
Stopping and giving them a
greeting card to share your heart?
Letting them know, that for
them you promise to never part?
Giving of one's self through the labor of love is an astonishing, caring
thing.
It causes a song deep within the heart, It causes the soul to joyfully
sing.
Love has only a beginning, Love has no end.
What does such a simple word
as Love mean to you?
Is it something you choose to do?
Yet another word that go hand in hand with love, is friendship…

# What is friendship?

Sharing hearty laughter with
someone you feel connected to?
Offering them a bit of sunshine,
when they feel blue?
Words spoken from your heart that
is offered as a precious gift?
Walking with someone in the park, talking
and laughing just because they
needed in their spirits a lift?
Holding that special friend's hand and
sharing each tear with them,
because they mean so much to you?
Isn't that what friends really do?
Or cheering boldly at a baseball game and sharing a hot dog and a
cold drink?
Or telling a joke just to see them laugh—you turn, look at them and
wink.
All the gifts of life should be celebrated together with a smile,
with sparkling eyes that ring of laughter, yes that laugh, love, and
live.
It gives us the real desire from
our hearts to truly give.
Love and friendship walk hand in hand,
it is in itself a marriage
that cannot be broken,
cannot be beaten down.
The laughter of true friendship,
has the most amazing sound!!
True friendship, if it is true indeed cannot and will not be destroyed.
Love that is real has no end, only a beginning. It lives on until time is
no more.

*Cathy L. Kaiser*

It grows in strength, it causes such hope, it becomes such joy,
and from that it will soar!
It thrives for an infinity and lives inside of each of us without an end.
This from my heart, this from love deep within me, this from my
deepest
friendship that to you I wish to send.

# Yes Free Indeed!

Jesus, in the name of Jesus—
Shall I remain free!
Yes free, in His very name, Jesus—
Jesus—Jesus!
All because He loved us so,
He died upon the tree
He did that just for you, He did that just for me!

**Jesus, in the name of Jesus..**

He gave us our hearts sight, Love,
Joy, and Liberty!
Oh yes, oh yes in the name of Jesus
He set us totally free!
Yes free, in His very name,
Jesus—Jesus—Jesus!
Because of Him, my soul has
a deep and joyful song!
Because of Him, I can truly say I belong!

**Jesus, Jesus, Jesus.**
**Yes free, in His very name, Jesus!**

I was traveling in a lonely place, a place that was so bare,
My soul felt so troubling, that it did at my heart's door tare.
I looked up at the stars one night, to look for something more,
that was when I saw the amazing joyous light!
Oh yes that was the day,
that I was given my truest sight!
When I said to Jesus,
I need something more than I have
I need something that no one else has ever been able to give.
I need a much better way to live.
He smiled so gently as He
took my hand that day

Somehow I knew He would
show me a much better way.
That is when He showed me Himself and His lighted path that I could
go.
And since that day, I have lived
for Him and loved Him so.
He gave us our hearts sight,
Love, Joy, and Liberty!
Oh yes, oh yes in the name of Jesus
He set us totally free!
Yes free, in His very name,
Jesus—Jesus—Jesus!
Because of Him, my soul has
a deep and joyful song!
Because of Him, I can truly say I belong!


**Jesus, Jesus, Jesus.**
**Yes free, in His very name, Jesus!**


So lift up your voice O people and sing!
Lift up your hearts and let your song ring!
Lift up your voice and give Him the praise,
Lift up your hands, to Him let them raise!
Yes, in the name of Jesus praise Him
with all your might,
Rejoice in his presence, bathe in His very light!
Praise Him with all your voice.
His joy is yours to have, it is your choice!
In the name of Jesus…


Mountains will move, troubles will cease,
Lives will be changed! Give Him your praise!
Give Him your pain! Give Him your joy!
Give Him your troubles!
Yes give Him your thanks
and ever joyful praise!
Worship Him, with your hands ever so raised!
He gave us our heart's sight,

Love, Joy, and Liberty!
Oh yes, in the name of Jesus
He set us all free!
Because of Him, my soul has
a deep and joyful song!
Because of Him, I can truly say I belong!

**Jesus, in the name of Jesus,**
**Yes free, in His very name.**

# You Are Never Alone

Do you ever feel disjoined and all alone?
Do you ever question if love
to you was ever really shown?
Do you ever feel that everyone is out of touch?
How you need to be held
and loved so very much?
Do you ever call upon God and feel your prayers bounce off the wall?
Do you feel that no answers come from your
desperate, beckoning call?
Reach out to Jesus right where you stand,
Reach out to Jesus, stretch as far as you can.
Reach out to Jesus and let your heart dance!
Reach out to Jesus, give
yourself a second chance!
Reach, oh yes reach out to Jesus!!

Jesus alone will engulf your
heart with love and His grace,
Jesus alone will bless you as
you touch His very face.
Jesus will fill you with His sweet abiding love,
Yes Jesus will fill you with His Love
Do you ever feel so dark and empty in the depths of your essence?
Do you ever feel that no one really ever hears your daily confessions?
Do you ever think all have abandoned you
and your relationships have all decayed?
Do you ever think,
you travel down a lonely road,
and say, "well for me, it is just the way."
Do you ever feel that all
is without hope and lost?
Do you ever feel that your efforts are all in
vain and your very soul was the cost?

Reach out to Jesus right where you stand,
Reach out to Jesus, stretch as far as you can.
Reach out to Jesus and let your heart dance!
Reach out to Jesus,
give yourself a second chance!
Reach, oh yes reach out to Jesus!!
Have you ever been in
the middle of total darkness,
no light anywhere in sight,
But yet see the clouds break and the brightest
beam come glowing through?
Have you felt that there was no way to
solve this problem and then
watch God unfold His answers?
Have you ever just didn't know what to do?
Then in the middle of the night,
God showed you the way,
He showed you everything you needed to do and exactly what to say?
Oh yes my friend, for you
He will always make a way,
He will always break the
clouds and shine bright,
until things feel better than okay!
He is only a prayer away,
one reach for the stars and you will find Him.
Jesus is waiting to give you that hope,
Jesus is waiting to help
you feel love and to cope.
Reach out to Jesus right where you stand,
Reach out to Jesus, stretch as far as you can.
Reach out to Jesus and let your heart dance!
Reach out to Jesus,
give yourself a second chance!
Reach, oh yes reach out to Jesus!!

*Cathy L. Kaiser*

# What Daddies Mean To Their Daughters!

What daddies mean to their daughters, no one else could ever know,
All the love, hugs, winks, and laughter that only daddies show.
How they can do anything!!
Every daughter does believe
Why, a daddy not knowing
how to do something,
is much more than any
daughter could ever conceive!!
My daddy's hugs and wink
of his sparkling dark eyes,
His word of honor served him best,
and to me never uttered a lie!
How wonderful was the life that
my daddy did truly live!
For it was hard to count all the blessings to me he did freely give.
No other could have given all
the things that he gave to me,
oh how special is that love that only Daddy has, and how it's meant to
be.
For when I needed him,
he grumbled then was there,
for inside he was all love,
outside kinda like a grizzly bear!

But that was all right with me,
for indeed I knew him best,
for he always was there when you needed him, always did he past the
test!
No one could do what daddies do for their daughters, no sir-EE!
No other could fill their shoes, like my daddy can! It isn't difficult to
see.

For daughters, daddies are just so special, that is the way God
intended it to be!
So often when I think of daddy,
I smile and am a glow!
For I remember my daddy and the love we shared—I know!
I know that today,
my daddy is watching over me,
I know his love still reaches me, and it still fits him to a "T".

**I love You Daddy!**

*Cathy L. Kaiser*

# A Glimmer Of Hope Right Where I Am

A sad, sad song, tears,
so many flooding tears shed
So many grieving things said.
Pain released, loved ones deceased
Feeling no hope, fighting for... fighting for freedom from dope
Having my life stolen from me,
some things happen,
somehow it seems was meant to be.
Feeling a slight glimmer of light, wanting to feel hope, yes with all
my might.
Urgently reaching and feeling
God's marvelous grace
Somehow actually touching His very face!

Feeling His grief over my severe physical pain
Knowing He does not give me any blame.
Trying to grasp His precious Love, His tremendous Honor,
His amazing Peace. Helping
my pain for a moment cease.
Giving me more than a glimmer of hope! Showing me His Great
Heart!!
Helping me understand from me
He will never abandon, never part.
Knowing how much I have yet to face, realizing what will get me
through
is tremendous love I can embrace.
Knowing I face a life in a
chair imprisoned by wheels,
Well meaning, good hearted people try to pretend they know how it
feels.
Knowing God can still reach me
even when I cannot stand,
Knowing His smile reaches across all the land,
Yes, right into my heart.
There I am no prisoner,

There I have the ability to be free!! It is a matter of choice, you see.
There in the heart,
I can rejoice and just be me!

*Cathy L. Kaiser*

# The Touch of Heart

Stars gleaming giving sparkling light
over shadowing the soul
with tremendous sight.
The sight of the soul gives incredible shimmering greatness
touching other souls in passing and in a moment once again, masking.
Painful suffering of the
body and heart sharing it all
with another is at the very least a start.

Touching lives with kisses of time,
giving the heart a tender love embrace of countless galaxies.
Not saying that there has never
been any fallacies.
Yet a trace, a trace of us that
shall remain throughout
the ages of time and space—Yes for infinity.

Growing with each other living our lives—giving, knowing
we have loved—we have touched—
we have truly lived.
Leaving our prints upon many lives, leaving our essence behind
to merely embrace love of life for infinity.
For after this life comes to its final breath,
what awaits us all,
is merely the next form of life to embrace, to love, to live.
Come, let's all continue in this journey together, in harmony.

# Not letting go

Open heart, full of tears
heart ache and bodily pains years,
so many years
Anger such a blaze of anger, fiery,
resentment, rebellious anger
not understanding the whys, not even understanding the questions
not understanding whatsoever.
Heart feeling severed,
set apart from all who care.
Looking at the view, who extend their hand
because they dare.
Losing all ability to rise, losing the heart
the heart that once had depth
once had caring that went deeper than the sea—once that was me.

But now just a glimpse of leaf blowing carelessly in the wind
once I stood strong and tall
just around the bend.
Why do I hang so tightly on,
and refuse to just let go?
These are a few of things I do not know.

# The Sight Of The Soul

Abandoned Laughter, tears of the heart
Rips of the soul, never seemingly to part.
Darkness falls freely over the sight of the soul
Mirrors peeking, tremors seeking
for what has been omitted, what has been lost
with such an enormous cost.
Sanity the price of the sight now seen
Breaking, splitting, tormented is now keen.
What is the price of the sight of the soul?

What is its ultimate goal?
How can I reach beyond this pain?
How can I hold my sanity again?
Body and heart aching—united as one
Body trembling, heart crumbling beneath the pain that it is now
making
Looking up one last time hoping,
believing to grasp
one shimmering light to hear one
note of a delightful chime.
Anything, everything, just one shred of hope.
Even just a morsel to help me cope.
Just when my head sunk low surrendering to the nothing, dark, empty
nothing
covered in darkness, engulfed in its emptiness
I surrender all I exclaimed as
my head slipped downward

But then, suddenly,
when all expectations were void
I heard a delightful one sweet note of melody
and felt the warmth of the
sun a tiny beam of magic
came through a crack above me
and gave my face a gift...

It gave me a smile,
a smile that seeped down to my very core
Just a glimpse of light, enough
to carry on and more
Aiding me to realize that
all things have its reasons
Everything has its seasons—destiny, destiny must play its part,
Increasing one's knowledge is just plain smart.
One thing you must keep close and one thing
you must always know…
How precious indeed is the sight of the soul

# Mirror Of The Soul

Mirror of the soul enlightened,
our lives lived with a design
Life lived with a caring,
throbbing heart, that is ever so kind.
Of all things together that cause us to become
our total selves with celebration,
With the greatest most
exhilarating anticipation.
Formed by flooding tears
and trembling heartaches
created by laughter and joy that reigns.
So much so that we never remain the same.

Life is changes, many changes, changes that shape us into being
changes that aids our inner
strength and growth.
Changes that causes our inner sight to sing.
Character building is not an easy chore
It comes with frustration, tears, and a lot more.
It also comes with strength, growth, satisfaction, and power when its
done
it reaps the deepest emotion and you no longer feel shunned.

# The Inner Heart

My inner heart moved, stirred, not disguised
open to new horizons, an offering.
In the greatness of my very soul, there is a great depth of urging,
yearning, imploring to be filled.
Eagerly awaiting to fill its own goal.
There in the spiritual place, in the depths of my very essence
I find I have a vastness, a place where hoping,
a place where believing lies,
where faith reigns!
This place is touched with unearthly kindness,
Kisses of mercy, caresses of grace—
heartbeats of love.
Bringing me to new heights of exhilaration.

There hope cannot tarnish,
it cannot be beaten down.
It can only be shaped, honored, adored
It sings a song with an astonishing sound.
It ignores life facts of despondency, it ignores truth of hopelessness,
despair, & grieving sorrow.
It quietly makes its way,
a road to hope, to love, to life—
that brings the heart an illuminating smile.
It delivers you to the direction
you sought for so long.
A faith springs up inside of you,
like an bursting flowing river
that shall never die.

*Cathy L. Kaiser*

So when hopelessness surrounds the world, and tries to steal all joy,
the peace that lies in the depths of the center of my being.
When desperation tries to give me a whirl.
I have to draw upon the very most deepest love, faith, grace, and
peace
that my creator without hesitation and constantly gives to me so
freely.
I sustain it, I savor it,
hold it close to my bosom,
as if it was my last breath drawn.
Because many times over and over, it is my truest salvation,
It is my hope, my light,
my strength it is my life.
It is that very thing that I cherish
it so very much
I will always graciously savor each sunrise
and continually with passion
celebrate each dawn.

# The Gentle Shepherd's Quiet Whisper

Deepest, Darkest Blackness of Night, gleaming, radiant, shimmering
stars of light,
illuminating amazing depth of spirit, igniting emotions to burst and
feel
Blazing fire of systematic view,
deep seeded, tightly sealed.
Things that my heart and soul always knew!
Never fearing total isolation from the truth,
the spirit.
Soul singing, celebrating with sound, grace bestowing without merit!
Love surrounds and abounds!
That solid Voice arrives with a quiet whisper,
adorned us with softness
of the sweetest chord,
For that loving spirit waits,
arms open, heart full,
eyes full of mercy, hands strong, but tender.
never abandoning, never wavering.
That gentle loving spirit,
always there, standing.

That Gentle shepherd is waiting,
quietly loving, right there.
Waiting… waiting, ready… ready for you to share.
That calling invitation always contributed,
mighty love distributed in magnificent form.
Loving, mending with so much depth, leaving not one, no not one
heart torn.

Know that it is always up to you.
It is something you must decide, it is something you must do!
It is a gift, a gift to you
from the heavens above.
It is given to you, with so much Love.
Reach out to receive it,

take the true gift of infinity,
reach for your dreams,
reach for your imagination!
The stars are within your grasp!
They are within your task!
Oh yes, the gentle shepherd has a whisper, a soft and sweet whisper.
Be oh so careful not to miss
its loving soft sounds.
Absorb yourself in all the love that from that gentleness does indeed
abound!
Oh yes, the gentle shepherd has a whisper.

# Reflections Of Your Inner Mirrors

Reflections of our innermost Mirrors
travels, yes journeys we take from the eminence of light.
Vision of aspiration, Soul of sight of inspiration
Self perception… Reality conception.
Dazzling, amazing light…
Calling upon our inward might.
Who we were… Who we are,
Who we are bound to become
Yes, the very beat of God's intimate drum.
Multiple layers… Our inner most spirit
Knowing… Believing…
Loving, the humanness of you.
Comprehending how joyous it is to share it.
All the questions… All the answers…
all the truths
of the universe and beyond
Contained within the very core of your being.
Enchanted with vivacious luster
from your very soul.
Stars glowing, moonlight gleaming,
heaven's gate beaming.
Touching miracles with new beginnings, yes touching God's very own
heart.
Somehow we knew from the very start.
Bathing in God's loving tears…
Dancing in His hearty laughter.
Knowing for certain there is a life ever after.
Gazing with all hope with depths of truth in life's own mirrors.
Looking for truth, for justice, mindful of the shimmering lights in the
sky,
The Realization is delivered. Lives lived before shinning bright, each
a star, for all to see, having no doubt, one day I shall be there.
Be there, among them,
one day, I shall be free.

# Listen With Your Heart

Does anyone really hear me?
Does your heart absorb
my soft spoken words?
Can your heart perk up
and listen patiently… quietly?

Listen, my friend listen… Listen with your heart.
Shhhhhhh… My good friend,
I know you are busy
but for one fleeting moment, listen to the stillness of my whisper
listen to it's very own distinct mark.
Tainted tears, sainted fears,
life journeyed, life loved,
travels walked, years talked, laughter spent..
Mercy with love… many times sent.
Wandered aimlessly,
body vexed with unlimited
startling, breaking suffering.
Searching, hoping for a covering of release. Does anyone really hear
me?
Does your heart absorb
my soft spoken words?

Can your heart hear me?
Listen, my friend listen…
Listen with your heart. For one moment listen
Listen to the stillness of my whisper,
listen to the whisper.
Mirrors watching, Hearts comprehending
Passing years, History of shame
I no longer stand the same.
Reality of heart, Dreams running rapid,
dreams causing me to feel,
who really knows which is really real.
Dreams hurling with energy

carelessly in the cool wind.
Yes for all the ages of time
and space without a sound,
without a moment lost, rambles in the wind.
Reality or a dream, sometimes one in the same, or it does seems.
Wandering, floating, fading in the wind, unseen by the unveiled
sparkle of the eye, it belongs to heaven,
for it has no capability to lie.
Does anyone really hear me?
Are you awake or fast asleep?
How can you be sure?
Which should you cherish the most? Which should be your
aspiration?
Which should be your inspiration?
Reality... or a dream?

*Cathy L. Kaiser*

# The sweetness of it all!

I Get lost in your sweet fragrance, by closing my eyes and drowning
in the beauty of its very own delectable fumes.
It causes every fiber of my
being to float on the notes
of the melody of your soul.
It plays its very own tunes.
My essences sings from
being in your mere presence,
in fact that in itself, is to me
the greatest of all—present!
My heart delights in just one touch of your skin
your smile kisses my very heart, it cause such incredible gladness.
It shields me from the lonely madness!
How you silhouette the sunrise, graced with more divine enlighten
beauty,
How you procure the sunset, blessed with more timelessness.
How waking up becomes invigorating episode.
How every moment of life with you seems
full of sight of the soul,
full of music of the heart,
full with energy of lust,
and over flowing love of life,
How I am indeed blessed from the stars above
to have the gift given to me—such a wife.
A wife indeed bestowed with so much love.

A life that has bestowed with so much cheer.
A life given so graciously without fear.
You give my heart so many notes that need, that crave to be played.
You make all the pain of life slowly,
eventually fade.

How my heart sings the
song of I love you always.
How it sings it invariably,
every day, all day long.
Form the heart, it chimes it without ceasing
yes from the very heart, it sings our song.

*Cathy L. Kaiser*

# The Silent Love Of Truth

I sit in the silence in the darkest of nights, the stars quietly
glimmering,
in it's place so tidy and neat.
I meditate without even moving,
embracing the hour of stillness
yearning for its greatness to
consume me right in my seat.
So still, not even the
beating of my heart present
the quietness of the depth of love that is there,
the sharing, the love with true depth, and all of it's tender care.

The stars glisten bright without one
tiny sound brought forth to my ears, in reverence of all
the love my soul has found, with respect of the many spent tears.
The fact of how my heart
longs for that love of truth,
love of heart, love that cannot
be compared with any other,
yearning for that special touch that reaches down in such depths
of my very inner essence, my deepest spirit
that very part that makes me sing, that knows only grace not merit.
That makes my heart soar
with bountiful happiness,
such joy lighted with incredible fire of yearning.
my very soul with truth of love has become
entirely vivacious with energy
that has fed me from such
truth of light, truth of love,
truth of the purest joy,
of the purest delights, it has kept me close to you, and not away
turning.

This I have known from the very beginning, yes from the very start.
This I have cherished with all my might, this has been at times bitter-
sweet,
but even still not churning to tart.
I have known that the yearning
was not for one fleeting moment
left on the surface to sit,
to fester in darkness alone
it has rather, soaked down
to the very core of who I am,
of who I have become, who I have always hoped with all my years to
be.
This is a sight of love,
sight of truth, sight of all hope—
that can never be blinded.
This love that was always
meant to find it's way home
to find it's last mile traveled, home where it belongs, home to me.
Where I patiently await with an open heart, and open loving arms.

*Cathy L. Kaiser*

# The Phoenix rebirth!

The Phoenix ruptures from its own ashes
rises to be reborn with enthusiasm to the vivacious, majestic sun.
He gives us all graciously the wisdom, the strength in our hearts and
our minds,
to feel in the depths of our very essence,
to make for himself a treasure, a most incredible find!

The great Phoenix soars with all his might to the heavens above,
in all of his miraculous splendor, he bathes in God's never ending
love.

His adventures of obtaining the impossible, his belief in the rising of
magic—
belongs to him and causes
us to have it in our claws.
It aims us to have a brand
new look at even our flaws.
Adventures, hope, belief in magic,
a smiling heart,
he is the keeper of all these things, perhaps a joyous keeper of our
very spirit,
the mirror of the soul, the sparkle of eyes that reflect so tender,
that pays to our merit.
Or at the very slightest,
it is an electrifying start.
It causes our inner essence
to sing a song that rings.

Rising up, rising high above all adversities,
Learning from history, assembling wisdom, gathering facts.
Busily making his nest from all the right twigs, for another grave he
does not dig.
Having his task set before him, believing his chores contain nothing
more to lack.

He wears his blinders snug, for his obtainable goals are oh so very
clear,
to improve his perceptions, his sight of the soul, his sight of destiny,
yes sight from our depths
within and without any fear.
His sight is in sun, so visible
without one speck of density.
So my friend, do not let
your tears burn on to your pillow tonight,
rise up learn awareness from past adventures,
let them burn a glowing endless fire,
and let it kindle bright.

To know, to learn, to embrace wisdom to change your destiny,
is to live with honor, to entirely be engulfed in
indisputable intelligence, bathing in truth and wisdom within.
Know where you have been,
know who you are,
know the truest path to make that excursion, and know just how far.
Know your righteous avenue to stride upon.
Know how to pause at the sun, at the morning light's first dawn.
Know when to embrace
the tears that burn deep inside,
and above all know
when to preserve the laughter,
that in your very depths, does indeed abide!

*Cathy L. Kaiser*

# Start Where You Are

Do what you can, start where you are,
The keys to the answers aren't really that far.
Progress, results are caused
by steps taken one at a time,
Honesty, willingness,
courage to take those steps,
the results will be victorious,
you will see, it will be fine!
Prayers sent from your soul right by your bed,
Your hopes, dreams, and all your desires,
the stars above sprinkled
its dust upon your head
Changes made one step at a time,
knowing, believing,
assurance that can be so kind.
Life is all about changes and taking that risk that holds a price.
Pleasures, laughter, sadness, tears, happiness and yes even our fears,
We experience them all
throughout our lifetime of years.
Embrace that moment of love
that will not let your heart go,
that lingering kindness
that reigns in your heart,
it shall guard you against each and every foe.

It is a gift, that is very clear,
a gift of love, that you keep close to your essence, keep it near.
Hug on to that gift, it is given so freely without the slightest
hesitation.
With an open heart giving
your all for that final destination!
Do what you can, start where you are.

# Fact or Fantasy?

What makes Fact a Fact? What makes Fantasy a Fantasy?
What makes a dream a dream? What makes our world so real?
What do you see? How do you really feel?
Open your mind, widened your eyes, look at your own truth, and find
answers to
those questions that lie secret in your depths.
Those secret questions you
have so quietly kept.
Is it belief? Is it speech? Is it a tangible thing to everyone?
Is it what everyone else sees? I mean just so you don't feel shunned.

### Fact or Fantasy?

Perhaps it is in the conception, a place that you call upon with a
profound cry.
a place that is yours—and yours alone. A place that you call your
own.
Open your eyes, at least give it a try.
Is it mere illusion because all others do not partake the same world?
Or perhaps it just the space that makes only your own humanity swirl.
Does a parallel universe exist by its own construction?
Or only by your very own acceptance?
It is the result of each person's deductions.
### Fact or Fantasy?

Does stars of such a dimension flickering gleam in an immeasurable
sky?
Or perhaps by the enchantment
of your own desires?
Perchance it is there to ignite your fire.
Does that greatness of such a vast universe hold honor, truth, justice,
possibly marvel of a bouquet of fragrance?
Or just maybe you spoke that world into reality, your own conscious
agent.

It is up to you, to look for the unseen,
unheard, the mystical
or are you…to be over
concerned with congeniality.
Is it a spiritual phenomenal
abode or is it mostly physical?
Each have their own roads to travel,
their own questions to search for,
their own answers to find, their own experiences to seek,
hoping that some of them will at
least be oh so very kind.
So, stay true to yourself,
stay focused most of all,
bathe yourself with honor and always stand tall.
There many worlds of worlds
in this vast universe of ours,
know that you shine in everyone of them
as long you allow the shower of truth to reign.
Then and only then, fact and fantasy, just perhaps could be one in the
same!

# Threads of Truth

Strands of truth, grains of character, rain of honor, mirror of integrity
pinned beneath our guarded shadow, beyond our very keystone
in the stillness of our soul, where it
silent, dark, and alone.
Our heart lurks in the midst
of our shadow, now stone.
In this life, and in our lives past, still, we seek to wear our well-fit
hidden masks.
We think our lips is not a
resting places for lie upon lie,
Yet bountiful, blended
there remains a haunted cry
Yet truths spoken in part,
at the end of each day.
Perhaps the Truths in Part
are just easier to say.

Is it an addiction? Is it soiled fears?
Is it something we have all just done, for way too many years?

Look around and you will see, it is in the newspapers, televisions,
magazines,
so simple to say what people want to hear,
truth becomes harder to hold,
as we want it to grow near.
It is true when it is said,
The Truth shall set you free!
I would rather have the uncut truth
and let a few tears shed.
Game playing is tiring, I shout I will not play!

So many so good at lying though… I hang my head low to say.
How can we possibly think that a part truth, is not a well spoken lie?
How we can see the whole picture, with missing pieces just out of our grasp?
Perchance this could be a new beginning, truths spoken in fullness, that will for many lifetimes last!

# Life's Terms

Reaching for the stars one last time,
Reaching for hope, believing
that God is ever so divine.
Knowing all it takes is trust in
Him to take that next step.
Knowing He can heal your heart,
love you with such depth.
Grabbing onto the end
of the rainbow in the sky,
grasping to the answers of the questions, yearning to know the whys.
Not always knowing in full, of why things are.
yet knowing that God's everlasting
love isn't very far


Understanding with clarity that this life is only one small part of
things,
Allowing the flowing music that abides in my depths to sing—to
forever ring.
Celebrating life on its very own terms,
accepting the lessons of what I must learn.
There are many roads to travel
and many places to go,
there are many to be blessed with, many things others to me can
show.
I accept all the challenges
that life has to offered me,
I accept it all and am grateful,
just simply to be me.

*Cathy L. Kaiser*

# Freedom Bought For A Price

The moonlight branded my passage, giving vision to unseen things
I see a single solider, that has a
song he is yearning to sing.
His sorrow tells a story,
so true but filled with grief,
all about how we have lost from our memory
the freedom he died for—
that made his life so very brief.

He paid the price for us all, with his own retching blood, his uniform
still wearing,
torn and stained with mud.
The hollow of his worn face brought shame to my inner core.
Knowing I had forgotten the price he paid, it seems like I had known
this before.
Freedom once dressed in honor and bathed in all of the splendor of
Victory!
Now torn, forgotten, lost, abandoned in our very depths
for soon to be a half century.
Tears poured from my soul, as I felt that soldier's tremendous grieving
heart.
He looked at me and had a partial smile, knowing it was possible,
that I had just made a brand new start.
Remember your freedom as you dance with delight on this very day,
it was paid with a enormous price, with blood, giving hearts,
with their very lives—yes, they did pay.
Open the sight of your soul, so you can see, open your eyes, your
hearts to a freedom, bought and paid for in full, for you and for me.

# Facing the Mirror

I traveled a very long journey and my body was urging for a rest.
I found a restful place—a huge boulder that would be fine, at least for
a spell.
I had this aching feeling that somehow in moments I would face a
test,
a test that would never be forgotten or one I could never repeat, or
tell.
I gazed at my feet and saw in the middle of the boulder, a glistening
glass,
In the very depths of my inner core,
I knew this was no
ordinary glass, a mirror, that it had a mystical aura, a magical mass.
In my heart, somehow I knew I was about to face an amazing thing,
something to cause my heart to cry out or sing,
I did not know, not as of yet, but it caused my curiosity to swell up in
my soul,
like a raging river, it was some sight to see, some sight to show.

I was compelled to look, as if the mirror itself called out to me,
as if it my heart already took, there I somehow it yearned to be.
I slid off that boulder and slowly,
cautiously walked toward it,
I could feel the intensity of fear,
or was it just anticipation?
It seemed as if I was called to this place, yes it all seem to fit.
When suddenly a figure that glowed with heavenly light appeared
before the rock, obstructing my view, and gave me
somewhat of a surprise …
… no… more like a jolting shock.
Her hand came up and she spoke
with a ringing sound,
I listened to every word as if the ultimate treasure I just had found!
*"Wait" She spoke, "Are you sure you want to look in this rare mirror?*
*For within it you will see yourself,*

*how you really are.*
*Your inner spirit may feel ajar.*
*The strong run screaming as they look inside*
*and the weak fall faint,*
*turning to death and ashes.*
*for they cannot handle the*
*depths within that abide.*
*For you see all of you, the*
*darkest parts to the very purest*
*This alone could bring you unlimited fears.*
*Or it could actually bring you the farthest,*
*throughout all of your years.*
*Only the most confident*
*and the most pure of heart*
*will stand true in front of this mirror, and are able to obtain its very*
*keys.*
*Most cannot handle their darkest side, they crumble and their hearts*
*fade away.*
*For when faced with their own evil, they shake,*
*they shiver at the mere thought of it,*
*they run with all their might, they*
*are just not capable to stay.*
*For to understand the good,*
*you must look through the darkness*
*towards the light, towards the magnificent light.*
*So know for sure if you can look,*
*know this certain,*
*Know it before you pull back*
*the knowledge curtain.*

*Make absolutely sure you desire and need to look upon who you*
*really are.*
*Be certain, you really want to go this far!*
*If you can—*
*bountiful things for you are in store,*
*for at your finger tips will come all the desires of your heart*
*they will be yours as sure as the gleaming stars set in the night sky*
*above.*

*Then and only then will you desire for more!*
*But be positive, you can look at all of you, the dark and the light.*
*Before your eyes fall on its truths, be sure before it gives your heart*
*full sight"*


She faded into the rock, right before my eyes.
I wondered, do I dare look into this amazing mirror, should I even
try?
Do I dare to embrace all the realms
of realities unknown to the dark
and light corners of who I am?
Of who I have been?
Of whom I am yet to become?
Can I not only face them but can I embrace them as part of myself?
To within those realms make my own distinctive mark?


I always felt I knew I was kind, good, and pure, would this stand the
test?
Would I find it true or would I find I was actually very dark, evil in
fact?
Would I end up in duress?
The thought caused my very inner
essence to tremble.
I could see how looking in this mirror could cause the strong to
crumble
and run screaming, and how it caused the weak to fall faint and die,
how it caused them to death tumble.


So the confident and pure of
heart holds this mirror's keys?
My first impulse was to turn away,
surrendering to the fright,
to let me keep safe, from such taunting fears.


I wanted to just walk away, after all,
laid before me I had many years.
Just walk away, I told myself.
I turned away, but it sang my name,

81

I could hear it,
I kept looking back every few steps.
I stood there my head down,
not knowing what to do.
Somehow I had a deep seated need to gaze upon that mirror,
to really know myself was important, I wanted to know all things, not
just a few.
My eyes fell to the earth in deepest thought, they fell to the ground
below.
I knew what I wanted,
I knew I wanted to face my
deepest darkest sides of my soul, without wearing any masks.
Somehow I knew then that I could obtain the greatest
accomplishments,
the ultimate wisdom, and achieve my greatest most tremendous tasks.
I took step after step towards
this great mystical mirror.
My eyes slowly, cautiously
fell deep within its perimeters.

I could feel the electrical impulses to the very core of my inner being,
yet it almost felt that every part in my essence was given to sing.
As I looked deeper in the mirror, in my life, in the deepest parts of my
very soul.
I was amazed it knew everything, even my most secret goals.

I saw and felt my deepest hunger, all my incredible thirsts were there,
my deepest aspirations, ever single hope.
Even my lack and ability to sometimes cope.

Every corner did I search,
every corner did I find.
I needed to know, I had to know,
More I needed more for it to show!
Was I as pure and kind of heart
that I had always thought?

Was I really given to the good things,
as I was taught?
What would be the answers
you search so long for?

Would you gaze upon this mirror?
Only you can answer that question my friend, would you look?
Or would you walk away and live with the aching regret of wanting
to look but finding not the courage that it took?
It is up to you, what do you think
you would really do?

So my friend, what would you do?
Would you crumble,
your heart filled with fear and run?
Or would stay and refused to be shun?
Would you hold on to your courage to obtain all there is to know and
see?

Would you look boldly and
directly into the mirror and say,
tell what you know about me!!
Would you face it with courage
against your greatest fears
even if inside of it contained the hardest tears.
Would you discover things about yourself that you did not know
before?

Perhaps then you would feel the
incredible thirst for more.
Would you walk away never
to face that courageous chance
or could it be what lies ahead
waiting is really a buoyant dance?

Waiting for you to eagerly embrace that
consciousness of endearing voyage.
The choice belongs to you,
my friend, it's yours alone to make.
Let your choices show
that it was made for good
Let them show it was for you,
and for you alone to take.

# Haunted Tears

Tears of haunted waters, waves of vibrations,
lavished with distress, aged fears to confess.
Flesh devastated, consumed bone-crushing fragments paralyzed
with realm sundering torment.
Muscles in demolition,
bones in weak formation,
Depths of the soul in condemnation.
Hope, beliefs, dreams, & aspirations smeared with obscure darkness
no trace of sunlight, of moonlight
to brand the passage.
Death of life, Heart invaded ripping
the soul an enormous tear.
Tears of torment, tears of grief,
tears of dismay and tears of defeat.
Battle raged—Limbs losing,
tears expressed—tears fading,
heart in pieces—heart shading,
life glistened—life dimming.
Breath of life blacken slowly.
No might to fight, No more light for sight. Is there one speck of light
to see?
Is it possible there is one fleeting glimpse—In all creation among the
stars

——Just for Me?——

*Cathy L. Kaiser*

# Yearning Greater Knowledge

In the depths of the earth's great waters reaching to the lustrous moon
that flows with unspeakable splendor.
The gleaming stars reflecting such harmony,
a true melody of a vast
stunner of majestic nature.
Examining all thoughts of humankind endeavoring to venture ultimate
destiny
if systematic views and humanistic wisdom
at the end of time shall with strength stand,
With promising possibilities
that our inner hearts
will take on a higher journey beyond the stars, or if in fact we can.
That in the stillness of our truest energy in each mind and soul,
when all things are said,
when all things are done,
when at last, we gasp for the last breath,
when life is past,
when life as we know it,
becomes a mere memory
what then? What remains to be felt,
known or seen?
Is there even a glimpse of one particle left, worthy to be redeemed?

Will the wisdom that once reigned
reach beyond the clouds
and kiss Heaven's gates?
Or will the essence of our well-fit masks be our eternal mates!
Will humanity's beating heart
live through all time and space?
Will we feel the midst of ultimate knowledge brush against our face?

Will others hear our essence like a
whispering musical tune
in the wind as it blows?
What indeed will become our legacy of our human's hearts and race?
These are just a very few things,
I yearn to know.

# Splendor of our Love

The gleaming stars and the moon that brings its charm so bright,
From the depths of my inner revived soul with all of its splendor and
might,
speaks out and sings from my essence, a song that forever rings
through all time, space and
throughout the night
My heart knows our love in its full measure.
My heart has seen
our love's exquisite treasure.
My heart feels and embraces its dazzling beauty and generous grace
it caresses its truth, yes touches its very face.
My throbbing devoted spirit, my heart only knows of the
many good things and how
to sacrifice without thought.

My gentle heart for you only knows to glow its
wondrous, blazing light, for which it sought.
My love for you has the abilities to bring all worlds into just one,
It finds quickly its exact and pointed center, and its work is never
quite done.
My heart, my love, has no selfish scheme
and does with everything does consider.
My beating heart knows that examining all things in life,
there are only a few that really matter.
Love and the hearts combined, not all the other useless chatter.
My Laura, my sweet wife know I love you in this world and many
worlds to come,
Know my heart belongs to you for an endless amount of time,
Know that in the depths of my heart, plays a beautiful endless chime,

For I shall forever, always, only …
belong to you
this I shall know and hold up to always be true.
There is no one within my reach of friendship
that misses, that of you I feel this way.

My body is a mere vessel
to hold my love for you,
it over flows with ebullience
each and every day.

Know that because of you
the sun shines so very bright,
know that because of you the stars
glisten marking my path
in the middle of the night.
Know because of you, that the flowers give a fragrance that is so very
sweet,
Know how grateful I am on that very day that we did meet.

*Cathy L. Kaiser*

# Loving you daily

I gaze deeply in the stars tonight, and I realize many things,
I know of all the things you have given me, not just a simple wedding
ring.
You have entrusted me with your heart and your laughter too,
how your laughter rings in my heart, how it gives life to me a new.

Your sparkling eyes that gaze at me with that happy but hopeful look,
I only pray and wish you do know, in a wink my heart you took.
You give me everything with a hug and kiss each morning
then lying beside at the end of the day, what more could I possible
want?

What more could I need?
What more could I dream?
I have it all, just being with you, so it seems.
I hope you know how much I love you, each moment, each day, each
year,
I hope you know I will be right here for you, quieting each and every
fear.

I adore you, I love you, I need you, I want you is all I think to say,
but I will each morning and then each night, for this is for you, my
way.

# Tears Dipped in Darkness

Passage in the darkness
to grasp one bit of light.
One tiny glimpse of assurance, of hope in an endless, infinite, dark
sky.

Empty echoes fall upon my heart, abandoned my heart's callous deaf
ear,
they speak into the hollowness of the wind, with why … why …
why?
Whispers, softly spoken in spoiled decay,

It fades
into the darkness quickly
as poisonous haze in the sky.
I grumble out the wonder, a question as I weep, yes, with tears a
wrenching
melody do I sigh,
so many things remain unanswered,
so many questions still there, so deep…

Despondent, grieving, agonizing, pain-racked tears baptized in frozen
years
Broken, traced with shale of suffering, in itself there is no guilt nor is
there shame.

Actions of soil—of the soul, cannot,
will not prevent what it shows,
nor what it indeed knows.

What it knows is unspoken truths,
|resting in silence, for it is untold.
Quietly in waiting, for all knowledge, for the oneness of the truth to
become known, to slowly without enslavement to unfold,
To finally once and for all
know what has truly been sown.
Perhaps then, Perhaps only then, we can stand together tall.

# The Splendor Of Love

Out of the generosity of
God's spectacular creations,
out of his artist hands, painting great splendor,
mountains, valleys, sunsets, roaming hills, and birds that sing a song
that thrills,
the most tremendous yet
perplexing creation still explodes,
from the earth to the highest heavens to the very depths of us all.
It brings to our hearts, to our very spirits,
the core of our being, the most majestic call.
So simple, yet so complicated when touched by the human heart…
"Love".
So pure, so perfect, so simple,
so tremendously tender, within us,
it builds a temple.
Love is so fragile but yet so strong,
It creates between us all a bond
assuring us we do belong.
Love is capable to be filled with such strength
it can weather the most intricate storms,
It can go the distance, it can ride the turbulence of great length
it carries us through like a triumphant song,
never judging, it even embraces us
when we are wrong.

Love is so refreshingly tender,
it quivers when it is touched,
It causes happy tears to flow,
and means so very much.
Love causes us to tremble when it our hearts move and has tears of a
dove.
The magic of what it can hold, what it can do is unlimited… LOVE
The creation of all creations, a creation that does not have the ability
to end,

92

to die, is has no capability to stop, it causes the heart to smile, joy to
overflow,
and just when it is needed,
our hearts it does defend!
For our hurts, our broken hearts in time of need, it will carefully
mend.
Love springs forward through all time, all space to the stars of infinity
through the heavens of light, it brings
to us all in our crucial time
more forbearance, more might.

Love, such an unending perfect circle, No ending no start, it only has
heart.
Love has no flaws, there is no earthly beauty that could compare,
Willing in all things with you to share. It uplifts your shadow, your
soul,
It rejoices in all things,
in everything it does know.
Love wipes a child's tear, when he stumbles
Love helps him up with a kiss and a hug.
Love gives your heart that little warm tug.
It holds friend hand
and walks in the fog of tribulation
It knows never any commendation.
Love faces all adversities together and wins,
there is always one more smile
just around the bend.

Love holds hands and gives a grateful prayer
It knows the importance of not
being selective in gratitude.
It celebrates in great magnitude!
Love embraces your life as the Years roll by
you love, you hurt, you feel, your cry,
your heart feels broken,
but that loves never dies.
You never regret the love you feel and felt
you shared, you gave without

thought time and time again.
The glow upon your face as you remember
and feeling your heart leap with joy and melt.
Life cannot exist without love,
it is necessary, it is needed,
without it we would surely die.
What an intelligent,
yet creative, imaginative creation.
He created love,
so that we would need, crave, want each other.

Love is kissed by white satin
for it made from purity,
it is kindness that has been
blessed by honesty,
it dances in the presence of truth,
It floats to softly kiss the moon's glowing charm
with a most brilliant joy that shines
throughout many galaxies,
it shields us all from the dreadful harm.
It sings a song that many
choirs of angels tenderly commerce
with a majestic voice of a joyous heavenly tune,
that quickens our souls to be convinced. It is a song that all ears can
hear,
that all worlds and the heavens
can feel so very near,
it brings a treasure, a treasure to our hearts that we hold so very dear.
Carefully the stars and planets
were put in their place,
they all shined bright in the
night to know God's true face.
He kissed the starlight and
gave it a dazzling glow
to forever light our passage way,
so that we should know.
That most blessed, extraordinary creation
was created just for you and for me … LOVE

# My Soul's greatest Song!

A admiration to the other half of my soul, the part that made me complete, made me whole was my sweet, Laura. The sound of our laughter together gave me pleasure with such depths that no words in any language could express the true meaning that gave to us both. The quick glances that were given like a selfless gift was an astonishing love song played over and over. The life that was given by merely holding hands caused my very soul to be caught in amazement. Oh how I adored her, how I treasured all she gave to my heart.
I slowly looked up and I gazed into the mirror of her eyes… I saw my whole world there. I gave her a playful grin as I reached across the table and gently touched her fingers. Her fingers—so slim, so feminine, so graceful. Just the mere touch caused the very depths of my being to thirst, to hunger. Yes a hunger, a thirst that could not be quenched. An everlasting blaze of fire that no one could extinguish. It would thrive for many worlds to come. It would shine brighter and with more vitality than the brightest star in the darkest of nights. It is a beacon of our timeless love for each other. Souls that explode in unison for each other.
An explosion of ecstasy, that would live beyond the heavens, beyond the shimmering
lights in the sky.

Our appetite, our aching hunger of flaming emotion for each other would exists beyond time, it would thrive in the twilight, the place where souls radiate forever more. The place that hunger and thirsting reigns for an infinity. A place for happiness to build many worlds that will in the distance come to pass.
Oh, I have loved her so—even before my birth or before hers, for I have loved the very covenant of her, from time's first spark of light until time darkens to its end. It is a love that will never cease, it has placed its prints among the stars for an eternity. Our love makes a place for us, it is called home.
Home the place that our hearts govern, the place of love and safety, a place that laughter celebrates is presence, the place in which we

belong, home. My home is that place where I am melting in Laura's arms, when our hearts beats together as one, then and only then am I truly home.

She smiled at me, and gently pushed back a strand of hair that was in my eyes. I felt her drowning in the blue ocean of my fire for her, in the mirror of my soul. Not a word was spoken, for no words were needed. I took her hand and pulled her gently—close to me. Our lips found their way to glistening against the incredible yearning for our taste. To feast upon all the desires and ignited passion, which, was now, merely kismet. Now awaiting destiny as a part of the whole, for it would come, as sure as the sunrise or sunset. Time holds our hearts and fiery rhapsody now, and to that we would surrender our all.

# Listen, My Love

Harmony in distinction
Heartening chimes with your name
bringing forth to the sweet earth all around you
the soft sounds of the rain.

Your essence I have touched,
I have found
the mere mansion of your sweetness
is what I from you—crave
your name, your touch, your smile
your lingering kisses, your ignited passions
it brings a truly hearty smile to my soul
that is what causes me to rave!
That is what abounds from my lips
such ringing, such raised sounds!
It my heart does save!

I raised slowly my eyes towards the heavens
towards the stars singing in union
as liken to a magnificent angelic choir
ringing in my ears of my undying love.
I listen to the rustling tones of music
in the wind, so much to my soul does it send!

Listen my love, listen with so much care,
the stars that glisten, the worlds that tremble
because of how our love we do indeed share.
Listen, my love listen to the kisses of time
beams of sun rays that
gives us warmth and is oh! So fair
Listen to the heart beat,
listen to the song that does chime
Listen my love, listen

# You Are My Gift From Above

Two years ago, today—
on March 13th,
Hearts were melted into one
Vows were given without hesitation
Rings exchanged in complete adoration.

Lives connected for a true eternity,
in a way that no words could truly express
that only two hearts could really feel.
Breath-taking, alive! Knowing, really knowing
in the depths of my heart,
how the excitement,
the beauty is sealed with such reality.

My darling, you are my truest
inspiration of wondrous beauty
that shines as a beacon to my very soul!
This is what my heart truly knows.
You are my love, Art in its greatest form.

I lift my eyes and
my hands toward the heavens
in wonder of all His glory
and in all of His splendor
as His choir of angels sing.
My heart becomes overwhelmed
with such nobility, such beauty and grace.
How I embrace a longing hope
to simply touch God's truest, kindest face.
To let the song in my soul, ring.

Of all his enchanting creations
I can feel, and see,
I can embrace fondly,
and oh such sweet scents
I can take in and savor,
of all the things that I can feel, I can touch.
Oh yes, they all mean to me so very much.

In all of God's creations, you are to me
His most breath-taking gifts of wonder!
But yet, all that I have touched with my heart—
the most astonishing, the most tender,
the most gracious gift
that God has given to me

————Is You————

*Cathy L. Kaiser*

# Pieces Of The Heart

Devastated, thrashed,
severed, ruptured, spoiled
at the very soul, by great gnashed teeth
ripping, tearing,
consuming each piece asunder.
The sounds amazingly resemble bold, extreme lightening and thunder.

But by impostors on the outside, with smiles that sparkle a mile away.
Truths easily hidden by their actions,
for at least a season,
at least for a while, until today.

How can the aching, heart wrenching wounds
opened, vulnerable,
be measured by any means?
How can I hold any belief
in being from this redeemed?
How can I heal, mend
from such slaughtered act,
I long to know, just how I can get past
all of these tormented facts.

My heart is kind, my mind is alert,
smart and clear,
my soul is designed to
love over and over again,
It has never known such fear.
Forgiveness, grace and honor once reigned
within its perimeters
never to stop once it began.

But how? How can this be
when my heart lays in
millions of pieces, not knowing how to even pick them up.
Strength was always my fortress,
given from above
I have no knowledge on how NOT to love.
I have not be taught to hate,
Nor in the light of all these things
do I understand how to debate.

How do I get past my heart not beating?
How do I get past the absence of my seating?

My heart is filled with sorrow, and crumbling fears, anguished tears,
What Now? What now, will my heart do for the rest of my years?
Do I awaken each day like
nothing has ever happened?
Go on as if nothing in any way is wrong?
Do I whistle as I do my daily chores, hoping it will all just go away?
How can I sing in my heart, a broken song?
These are a few question my heart
and mind is wondering today.
I search in desperation for that person,
before the wounds
came in with a screaming darkness that person that got left behind.
That person, that for now,
I cannot seem to find.

*Cathy L. Kaiser*

# A New Beginning

Silent laughter, hushed by affliction—a short-lived condition.
Joy squandered, facing such sorrow—questioning tomorrow.
Hope, believe, celebration of life—fading
out of control, out of domain, out of reach,
nothing more to understand or teach.

Just when all seems so very lost
just when it becomes a enormous cost.
A price too high to be paid
just when the journey is to difficult to travel,
the journey before us that is laid—

The dawn erupts and diminishes
the vast darkness
diminishes the cloudy musk over our eyes.
Death no longer dances of joy in our presence!
A new brilliant sun appears to give a new illuminated day,
To give new breath,
new fragrances, new blooms,
a new chance, a new faith, a new smile, and a brand new hope.
Oh yes, a new day becomes reality, and hope once again is tangible!

**A New Beginning Is Born**

# Tranquillity Of Truth

Stillness of my heart,
the serenity of my essence.
The presence of tranquillity extends a hand
of majestic peace, ceaseless adoration, endless harmony
one that may not be purchased, one that cannot be earned.

It is an openhearted,
openhanded gift to only bestow
from the true depths of one's soul.
It is an offering of love,
that should be given in secret,
in an hour of silence, a moment of whispers.
An offering that moves the heart,
never giving it merely for show.

The stars that shine so bright
in the darkness of a vast sky
they sing a song of celebration,
dancing in the presence of truth,
giving a lighted passage to our journey.
Yes, walk in that journey,
take that rewarding adventure
by the stars amazing presence, the stars amazing sight.

Look closer, gaze into their lighted wisdom
with more inquisitive questions
with a brisk wonder lust in
your mirror of your soul.

Spark the questions that crave an answer,
take a glimpse in the widows of wonder
hunger for the answers
that hold on to only truth.

Reach for the purest form of truth.
Let your heart embrace truth in its fullness,
Sanction your sparkle to
radiate in the eyes of its purity.

Truth you can run to, trust with all your might,
truth you can bath in,
truth can give you honest sight,
Truth will protect you, give you shelter,
truth will ignite your spirit to an
unquenchable fire that reigns deep within.
Truth will make a stand, over and over again.

An amazing gift, one that from you
will never part.
Yes, stillness of one's heart,
truth's tranquillity of your very essence,
thriving, loving, giving you growth of character.

**————Truth————**

# Our Childhood Dreams

Our deepest dreams, our most silent kept hopes and treasured wishes,
time, space, are given to cherished kisses.
Kisses of time, kisses of hope.
Timeless, endless, immeasurable, boundless
given from our very heart, from the very beginning, from our very
start.

We grow older and leave
our child's dream behind,
we call them dust collectors,
with time they lose their shine.
we remember them, now and again,
and offer a hearty laugh.
Such silly dreams,
a child with full imagination can have!

But in the most secret place of our hidden treasure within,
we are urged to cling to
those childhood fantasies,
those dreams that we had back then.
We want to shine them bright,
we want so much to hold them
close with all our might!
We want decades later those
adventures to come to light!

Reach strong to those adventures once lost,
that can be found again,
yes, perhaps with a cost.
Reach toward the star light—
towards that child's laugher
that laughter that rings with
so much joy and grace

reach towards the sparkling childlike eyes and their amazing face!
Reach for the stars, my friend, reach for that
imagination, reach up as far as you can,
reach high!
Oh my friend, never let that child's imagination,
that child's dreams,
hopes, adventures ever die!

# A Fresh, New Beginning

Sorrow to celebration, tears to Laughter
Stillness to dancing, isolated to Embrace
Barren to birth, agony to Bliss
Hate to forgiveness
Death to life, Sunset to Sunrise

There is a time for all things, each having a proper season,
each having their special reason.
A time to cry, a time to laugh.
A time for sadness, a time for dance,
A time for that one, new special chance.

A time to journey to new life, to a new aim,
to live with new freedoms, releasing all previous chains.
Each to be celebrated in its own path,
in its own right, in harmony and Peace.

To at last give your heart its total release.
As the sun breaks and
rises above the mountains,
as the rivers flow, like a never ending fountain…
Welcome to your new beginning!

# Embracing The Now

From the first spark of light
at the beginning of time,
from the first star hung in a vast, dark sky,
to when the sun first kissed the morning dew,
I knew my heart belonged to you.
From seasons when
the planets were put in line,
from the day the angels
embraced the moon to shine,
from dusk until dawn when our presence visited our great mother
earth,
until rapture of emotions were surrendered, were given to mirth.
My soul knew, when we touched, yes it was you, always you.

Two souls, before the clock ever set,
before a word ever written,
would come together in love, in destiny and be for infinity quite
smitten.
Before a note ever played,
the songs would thrive,
Before ink would be found,
poetry would be tried.
For as long as the inner heart can be found,
joys, wishes, heart throbs,
celebrations of the soul
elated breathlessness
will ring the sweetest sounds.

My eyes have always seen you, only you.
My love, dance in the presence of all our joy, all you can hold,
Dance in delight, bath in our joy, before the night slowly turns so very
cold.
For all we really have is the now,
this very moment,
touch our undying love, hold it, squeeze it, give yourself to it with all
your might.
Open your eyes, so that you may be given fullness of sight.
Sight of soul, sight of love, sight of purity, sight of security of the
soul.


These are a few things, you all ready know.
For when our last breath is drawn, we shall continue in other forms
continue our love, in the starlight it will shown.
My life, my body, my heart for you, only you, always you, until time
is nevermore.

# Daily Victories

Daily grasping onto life
that gives both joy and tainted sorrow,
that gives the warmth of the sun,
and renders broken beams of light.
Tears lined with so much fright.
But yet there is a place,
yes a place…
that gives us hope for tomorrow.

Looking towards the heavens for hope,
for solutions beyond our imaginations
reaching for the stars and above
toward that one higher spirit that adorns us
with an incredible amount of love.
Reaching for a kindness that
contains no contamination.

That one huge hand that reaches down,
and brings us up from such a mess,
that reaches down with so much care,
and thinks of us—no less.

So when I think of days filled with gloom,
I realize hope is not far away,
that even though the
present is seemingly filled with doom,
a ray of sunshine is near, perhaps even today.

For where the darkness lies,
glory of light there too abides.
From sadness comes glory,
from glory there is a story.

Know from each part felt,
your heart will rejoice and melt.
Tears to laughter of the soul,
belief to what you really know.
Frowns of poverty to riches untold of smiles,
love, wondrous love that always reaches across the miles.

So with all of these thoughts well said,
with many a thoughtful
tear that has been shed,

I will reach my hand out to you,
with a smile, a heart full of love,
paid with a price, that has been well over due.

*Cathy L. Kaiser*

# A Glimpse Of The Heart

Outraged, corrupted, disgraced, precarious natures, treacherous
minds,
infected hearts that should of been graced by goodness, by purity of
light.
But yet the darkness set in, and caused our carnal desires run a muck.
And caused us to have dimmed views, clouded hearts, and tarnished
luck.

To only blame God for what we
ourselves have created,
our natures refusing accept any responsibilities it seems,
blaming is our only tool,
for our puffed up egos,
Humility the missing component
of our learning school

The complete sadness this must cause our creator, our ever loving
God,
for in his eyes his creation was complete
and had given His trust in our free wills, our freedom of choosing.

Yes trust that the bright pure
light would guide our passage,
and that our desires would
turn to goodness, and pure things,
that would cause a melody
deep with us to erupt worship
and a song from our hearts would we constantly sing!

Why do we allow the
depths of darkness to rule?
Why do we seem to make choices of a fool?
Then when all things are a complete mess, we call upon that light
and think we have done nothing—
more or less.

We think it strange when we see broken-hearted tears stream down
His face,
yet, what is ever so steady, ever so present of course, is His amazing
grace.

He picks up and holds us close, not holding back one bit of His love,
He gives all without hesitation, all the treasures from the heavens
above.
Would we be so generous? Even to our children, would we be so fair?

Ponder on it, if you dare,
if you dare to look deep inside,
to find what lies within.
Take a look with eyes of truth
what your heart contains,
So take a look, if you dare to see if your heart
is clean or perhaps a bit stained.

No matter what answer lies ahead,
there is one true fact,
that God in His loving mercy,
holds His arms out to you
with nothing inside to lack.

*Cathy L. Kaiser*

# Two Hearts Blended In Joy

In a crowded room—
A sweet, soft glowing glance,
hoping our eyes will meet,
or at least there is a chance.

A playful half grin, hoping
you will in my arms once again.
Erupted in song of sweet-scented violets,

Yes indeed, Violets Of Love
Showered from heaven's opened gates and windows from above.

In the very depths of our inner essence, there thrives an everlasting,
flowing pool of emotion and beliefs ignited by the greatness
of a explosion of love's components.
Those very components arises on the
wings of harmony deep inside two hearts
knowing there is never an end,
but merely a start.

They blend together, throughout all the ages of
time, space, and worlds that exist
in times past, present and those to come.

This is what causes our hearts to dance
in the presence of our joys
and our everlasting bliss.

This very thing causes our souls to sing!
I shall be forever be here with my arms open
offering you all my love, my heart, my life—with an adoring kiss.

# A Brand New Tomorrow

Smiles, laughter, joy—all silenced.
Tears streamed with haunted fears,
events filled with tainted nightmares, throughout all my years.

Heartache, sorrow, pain grieving troubles near,
heart, soul, essence being severally seared.
Reaching for that mustard seed of hope,
stretching high above for
that one gleaming star,
Oh my, how they do seem
so out of reach, so very far.

Just one flickering moment of a bursting cheer,
would be all that is needed to comfort the heart
that could cause the vision to be a bit more encouraging and clear.

I look to the west, than the east, to the north and then finally south,
yet dark, hazy, disappointment covers my soul,
and not one smile, nor sound of laughter comes to my mouth.

My spirit has no sense to
give up the "good fight",
it continues to search, yes it continues with all my might, to find just a
little light.

For when I obtain just one speck of torch, I shall grab on and hold it
so tight,
so close to my heart, I shall then know that there is hope
of a joyful laughter to ring again deep inside, and a chance for a brand
new start.
A chance for that cheerful song, to come alive in my very depths and
abide!

So know that the fight of the hopeful soul continues on until time is
no more,
I shall continue my faith, and keep knocking diligently at the prayer's
door,
I am sure that prayer is the key to all things that are good,
and that faith opens the flooding gates of all things that it should.

So when I feel my heart is filled with so much grieving sorrow,
worries, and perplexing thoughts that my smiles turn to tears,
I look to hope, I took to the stars, I trust
that the answers patiently
wait for me inside tomorrow.
My encouragement lies
in a brand new morning,
and that a brand new chance is near.

For the alternative is not a
choice as far as I can see,
not one I desire to allow in my life to simply be.

My greatest inspiration, my greatest aspiration,
is that laughter, joy, and true happiness shall return again,
and that my heart, my inner soul, my tainted fears, my haunted
dreams,
will at last, be able to
obtain a beginning to mend.
Oh to be given the spark back
in my eyes one more time,

to hear my laughter ring, to feel my heart sing.
Is the gift above gifts that
sound with perfect chime.

# Everlasting Strength

From our endless inner passion, comes a deep glowing greatness,
that fills the sky with perfect glory, overwhelmed with cherished
honor,
Lined with tears of joy, of happiness, yes, tears filled with innocence
of heart.
I stand alone with my creator,
it is not often "in fashion."

It contains grace with adoring security,
of love, of lively heart, of tremendous sight,
from the beginning, what shows
is a strength full of heart
yes indeed it shines and
has from the very start.

An amazing glowing light in the darkest of darkest of nights.
It comes when needed, for it is in the depths of our core, deep seeded.
It's the love you keep so deep within,
it's the light of the drops of your essence,
in the center of the abolishment of your sin.
When the light of integrity is allowed to reign,
where there is no not one
place for any stain of shame.

Where light only lives,
a celebration sings loud,
that place where no allowance for the dark
Yes that place where deep inside of you,
where God makes his own distinct mark.
That place where he gives you a song to sing
that place where no one else
can listen or hear a thing.

*Cathy L. Kaiser*

His Strength is from a
everlasting flowing fountain,
His love is taller than the highest mountain.
His grace reaches as far
as the east is to the west.
His smiling heart takes care of all the rest.

# Ahhh, Good Times Roll At last!

Intelligence without learning,
receiving without yearning,
drinking without thirst,
being blessed without being cursed
being first without being last,

last eating without ever a fast.
Bravery without fear, Joy without tears
laugher without cries,
success without many tries.
Victory without failure, loving without ever knowing any heartache,

Smiles, sadness, joys, failure,
victories of our hearts,
we understand, or least know in part.
Comparison of the good or bad?
How does one exist without the other?
How we know when to
be sad or when to be glad?
The comparison are like sister and brother.

How does the beauty of the
stars hold our delight
without its shine, its very light?
So when bad times roll by once again, remember the good times are
just ahead,
to remind you that the bad has its reasons, and that they only last a
season!

So hold your breath and travel through, say to yourself, I will do what
have to do!
Smile big and know it soon will pass to a better, a better road
to laughter with a loud proclamation—saying, Ahhh the good times
roll at last!

119

# Freedom In Our Love

In the very depths of the
center of my essence within
I find a harmony, a graceful song,
and where it does begin.
It sings of such grace, as my heart caresses your sweetness, your face.

It sings of awe of beauty
that no one can put to words,
more beauty does it posses than the graceful flight of the Phoenix
bird.
One who cares where she has been,
and the flight before her is merely hers to lend.
For it all works together, for the outcome around the bend.

Your beauty is my beacon
and does direct my path.
I love you more than words can tell,
because of it around my heart, there is no need for a hard shell.

You have given me more freedom,
more energy of life
than I ever thought could be,
you have given my soul more sight, more light,
for through your might, I have been set free!
The chains of life cannot hold me now,
for your smiles, laughter,
and kisses upon my brow,
have render my heart,
my life with so much glee,
that I have no need to take a flight to flee.
Thank you my love for all you
have given to my heart, my life
Thank you my sweet,
for becoming my partner—my wife.

And with this moment,
just let me say one more thing,
The song of my heart
will through eternity—Sing.

Your name it will ring, and ring out through the stars and over the
moon,
For I know we shall cherish our love, and our song forever will play
its tune.

# Voices From Beyond

Our consciousness.. Full of promise, unclouded, spoken words of
saving grace,
hushed tones, out cries from beyond death—beyond the grave.
Whispers of hope, endeavoring to reach out to us and from ourselves
save.
A whisper from the past, soft in tone, but yet spoken with such clarity,
a portal to obtain the opportunity to touch our creator's face.

Ready and willing to heed to the magic of belief, yes, whispers of
hope,
assurance in our cries beyond what we understand—beyond what we
know.
Reaching out to the soft
tones of enchantment, reforming
our hearts, aiding our skills to cope.

Engaging in teaching us
what previous years did they sow.
Giving themselves to God's task,
to us do they strive to show.
Do we hurl those echoes of the long ago past, distant truth
to the stars that glimmer in vast moonless sky?
Do we create them as castaways,
cause them in darkness to lie?
Perhaps our choice is clear, if we pull them close to our very hearts,
that would be a radiant beginning,
at least a dazzling start.
Listen to the voices, speaking,
whispering in our very soul,
for those soft whispers may
just save us from more than one woe.
If we heed to those voices that
walked before us long ago,
such excellence, such significant purpose,
an amazing profit, their lives could show.

Listen to whispers that have
chosen to aid our travels,
Allow your heart to view the
splendor of such inner sight,
Let's welcome the eye of our soul to be blessed with God's amazing
Light.
Yes my friend, Listen to the whispers,
that cry in the night.

# When I Am Alone With You

I adore a starry, dazzling light in the darkest of darkest nights…
I love your sweet face in soft candle light
when I am alone with you.
I cherish rainy nights sweet melody pledged from my heart.
Knowing that in the vastness of our love, this only one small part…
when I am alone with you

I have the world at my fingertips, when we walk hand in hand…
I love to hear you laugh with our toes playing in the sand,
When I am alone with you, Oh baby, when I am alone with you.
I see the sky that is filled with our dreams.
Life is always much more than it really seems,
Oh yes, my darlin, when I am with you…
All my dreams, all my fantasies, with you always come true…
when I am alone with you,

My darlin, when I am with you, everything seems so bright,
so full of life, oh yes everything is so right.
Oh baby, baby, when I am alone with you.

# Kisses Of Time

Drops of my essence kisses time of infinity,
as I travel in the vastness of the universe,
as I hold the flickering stars
of glory in my hands,
as I understand truth, and each little strand.
As I am given sight to purity, to honesty, to grace and its love in its
fullness,
The road that it plows, I understand to a heart's sight to distinction.
That I see with all clarity,
that my sight is in fact nonfiction.

To know ... to love ... to live
... to just simply be,

To long for...to hunger for life of honor ...to offer myself to honesty,
to show my heart,
to celebrate each day of living,
to cherish each waking moment,
to devote myself to caring, to dance in the presence of each joy, this is
what I see.

To offer my inner spirit to soar in freedom, in truth, in love's very
light,
To reflect with each step taken in purity of the heart, in the eyes of the
soul,
to discover that the energy that grows deep within, becomes my very
might.
The energy of fight that is ablaze in my depths, that I can feel, that I
know.
To finally let go of all the emotional baggage that I have for so long
towed.

To bathe in the fountains of truth, to dance in the presence of my joys
that I feel,
to comprehend that the caressing of space, time, and infinity is ever so
real.
that dimensions that
can only be seen with the third eye,
the reality that can
only be glanced at with courage,
taking a look at my inner essence,
a look of true substance,
this is living with all I can be, knowing truth without surfaced lies.

This is a start to glory, to a blazing reality of excellence, an open heart
of purity, bathed in truth, in sincerity, in love's fullness of light,
This is my very drops of essence,
my inner eye's full sight.
What does your third eye, tell you my friend?
That eye of the soul, the eye of your dimension of depth, so deep
within.

# Haunted flesh

Tormented, haunted flesh in adversities
bound in agony with no release in sight,
no door of hope, no window of grace,
no tears of joy, not even a trace.

I sit in this prison, a chair bound with wheels
if only I could touch God's tremendous face.
And bathe in the joys, that once was so real.

No abilities left for battle,
no energy for the fight,
darkness filled my world,
no room for anymore light.
I wake each morning to know the
pain will be there,
to know that my life with it I
have been made to share.

If only I could focus on the joys
laid before my feet,
if only I could feel once again,
that this I too can beat!
It taken my body and my in heart
it has stolen my song,
it taken my mind, yes I know that is wrong.
If only the sunshine for a moment
I could hold in my lap,
even only I didn't feel that
this was the ultimate trap.

I could soar with eagles
and spread out my wings,
I could find that special place in the stars and from my heart sing.
I could be free within myself, where nothing could touch me there,
I could at last be have liberty, and not vulnerable or bare.

So in the depths of my spirit which once was full of light and liberty,
I shall capture that light once
again and let it reign in me.
It shall set my soul on fire,
a blaze of victory shall give birth,
so that I can again be free, and experience truth of gladness and mirth.

# Horror Of Shame

Haunted dreams,
Tormented realities,
Fantasies untouched,
Tainted drops of essence
Sanity slowing stumbling,
Mind commence mumbling.
Invaded shadow, hallow spirit
Echoes of consciousness, falling on deaf ears.
Magic of hope dimmed
throughout all my years.

Fantasy of faith slowly, gradually fading,
The moon glows no more,
The star's light loses its glimmer, they shine less than before.
Insight of the shadows in
the darkness of the night,

Taunted absent memories,
lurking clouds of mystery,
Storms of thought, storms of deed,
storms of misery,

Taken the late hours of the darkness, burning of the midnight hour,
Causing the corners of the soul to sour.
Prisoner in my own body frame,

There must be an escape
from this horror of shame.
Walking in the hallways of hollowing darkness to face realities
untamed.
No passage before me, just haunted cries in the shadows of blame.

# Magical Freedom

Soar like an eagle, ride on the glowing moon,
Know the laughter deep within, will see the heavens soon.
give your heart to the winds above,
give the smiles of your soul to love.
Grasp onto the melody of the magic star,
come on reach higher it isn't really all that far!
Do what will in the face of your grieving pain,
Come on! Reach a little higher!!
Ride that star again!
Let that laughter ring and ring,
give your heart to twirl and sing.
Find the magic in the depths of your core,
know the music, like once before.
Give yourself to that magical touch,
Come celebrate the things you love so much.

# In the Starlight

Beams of invigorating light
A mindful sparkling presence
A charismatic structure of might

For heart beats of greatness
For breathless gasps of distinction
Guidance by starlight knowing
without one single doubt,
that here I face no discrimination.

Before the moon fades into the dawn,
Before the darkness diminishes
into the day's light,
I shall have my soul's
perplexing query answered

My path of my journey shall
be once again be bright,
My heart once full of darkened shadows, shall be given full sight.

All before the sun and the
moon pass each other's path,
For a brand new morning, a brand new day,
Reach up to the sky! Smile at the sun!
Kiss the morning dew,
For once again we have yet another chance,
For today, we are given a gift, we have another day that can be
renewed!
Once again, there time to Sing! Once again there is time to dance!
Once again our hearts can sing a song that rings! Once again there is a
chance!

# Majesty Of Space

Time, the universe, the majesty of space,
its far more incredible
than any sight can envision,
any imagination can dream,
far more mighty than it ever seems,
it has no divisions.

It journeys to infinity, beyond what
any eye of scope can see.
It is more than my mind
could ever comprehend
or my heart could possibly adhere to,
After many miles of traveling,
we know it is eternity's key.

The moon's glowing, enchanting beauty,
the glory of the glistening stars
they know with nature's smile and sparkles at their honorable duty.

In such a tremendous space,
a vast, unlimited sky,
we are in our Father's presence
blessed with His giving grace,
we, being so insignificant, yet being so precious, a cherished race.
We find finally that we are not alone, the stars will sing if we can
listen,
the wind whispers, the planets breathe
and time and space with love it does glisten.
The whispers are there, hush my friend, listen, we are not alone.

We are loved—we are connected, from the first light of the stars
from the breath breathed into man and woman from the beginning of
time
from the first rain drops had fallen,
We have never been alone
bring it close to your heart, hold it, love it, know the whispers of the
wind,
from the enchanting glowing of the moon, and the gleaming stars
again,
We are not alone,
we have never been utterly alone.

# Reflections Of Freedom

My eyes behold the splendor of the infinite star lit sky and its burning
glory.
it quickly brings a smile of
contentment across my face.
As I gaze with amazement
I see the gleaming stars
and vivacious moon that is brushed with exquisite taste.
My inner heart engulfed in great kindness, has many stories to share,
so many enchanted places have I seen,
have I touched,
the journeys I have traveled,
has taught my heart to place
no rules or conditions when
I give all my love and care

With whispers of the gentle winds,
sweet, harmonious chimes
of the planets does send.
In the waves of the magical, frosty,
blue waters of the ocean,
a mere, single reflection appears,
it gazes back at me.
Hollowing inner depths am
I now capable to see,
beyond the waters, a shiny metal object,
half hidden from me,
I reached and held it carefully
in the palm of my hand,
gently, from it, I brushed away
each grain of sand.
Just then, I smiled with a most pleasing but puzzled look,
it was a key, I reach down and took.

I realized instantly it was not just a key, it was not ordinary by any
means,
I knew it was about to open the doors to pathways of adventures for
me.
My heart was certain as if I had been here, at this place before,
some how I just understood things, from the very depths of my inner
core.
The key was inscribed, "Courage to unlock your own prisons!"
I sat back and smiled, for I knew that this key
it would open the elements in this world and many worlds to come,
I would embrace it all before I was done.


Adventure after adventure I shall occupy the substance of truth and
freedom,
not causing my own prisons,
not building the walls,
not trapping myself and taking my own falls.
I will soar among the eagles, and shine among the brightest stars in
space,
I will feel the moon's glow gently upon me, and with all her brilliant
grace,
I will boldly look upon that reflection, clearly see my own inner soul
and face.


Now that I have the key
and the direction to take,
finally true sight and freedom is mine to make!
The journey to free myself, is a choice of courage you see,
To take that first step, and simply just be me.

# The Inward Eye

The undercurrent depths of my spirit journeys me to a serenity
that cannot be declared with words or actions of any physical sense.
Despite the obvious joys that appear from within with a pleasant
smile,
the fullness of harmony that flows from the depths of my core
commence!
My journey has brought me to many places, my feet have tread many
a mile.

The waves of peace that lap
inside my heart and mind,
I have searched diligently,
my whole lifetime to find.
Though at times, trials and hardships had presented themselves in my
path,
as bursting storms with roaring thunder all around me, in an angry
wrath.

I pull within myself to find that place, that place of sheltered warmth,
that special place of inner peace of the heart that keeps me still,
It offers me a tranquil focus to know what is important and real.

How so often we lose ourselves in the storms that rage all around us,
when the important things of our hearts and lives get so lost,
oh, how my heart does
grieve that enormous cost.
Our focus gets lost, our goals get jumbled,
The most important things and people in our lives get fumbled.

If somehow, we can
keep our eyes on the center,
If we can remain, our soul's greatest defender.
If we can keep that eye,
where it does indeed belong,
If just somehow, we can not drift from singing our heart's delighted
song.

To not let life events drift us from the truth,
To not falter, from where
they yearn so much to be,
If only right then, we could allow
our heart's eye to always see.
Yes indeed, our inward eye that pleads for our most clearest sight,
we must keep it focused, gleaming in the inner depths of our spirit's
light.

# Welcome The Dance

In the face of sorrow, even when the uncertain of tomorrow,
when your world around you crumbles,
when your health takes a dangerous tumble.

Let your heart dance!
If you have a chance,
dance, my friend, dance!

Even when your pain taunts you,
even when you do not know what to do,
when all forsake you in time of need,
when you fear, there is no one to take the lead

Let your heart dance!
If you have a chance,
dance, my friend, dance!

When your tainted tears hit the ground,
know in your depths of your inner sight what you have found,
When you bellow against the clouds an enormous sound,
and you feel empty and your insides feel torn and down,

Let your heart dance!
If you have a chance,
dance, my friend, dance!

Dance when things are sad,
Dance when you are glad,
Dance when everything is hectic and things seem to be a muck,
Dance when you are blessed with good fortune and luck!

Dance in good times and bad,
Dance with courage, with all your might,
Dance in the presence of the moon and the glowing starlight.

Celebrate all facets of life
with a joyful dance of your soul,
Claim your peace and let
the pain of your body and heart go!
With open arms and an open heart welcome yourself to the dance!

*Cathy L. Kaiser*

# We Are Never Alone

The planets slowly drift
among the stars so swift,
the glistening light erupts
in the deep darkness of the night,
The moon burns a glow,
that seems to obstruct your very sight,
All the things we need to journey, and to give to us a peaceful light.

The eye of the needle,
views a whole new
dimension of time and space,
it brings forth a new reality that causes events to gently fall into place.
We see ourselves detached and alone,
greater than the truth,
or the world we stand upon.

The eye of the needle
show us we are not single or alone
we are insignificant yet,
more precious that a diamond stone.

Nature's winds roar around us,
pedals of roses float as feathers at our feet,
aroma and beauty is simply ours
to every early morning greet.

Knowing who we are,
and where we shall tread,
is the task before us, we have read.
The one thing we must know—we are truly never alone.

# Embracing Hope

I embrace the great skies, so full of knowledge blessed by the
starlight.
The wisdom of the planets and all they obtain,
Knowing God's very spirit has in this place always thrived and
reigned.

I yield my heart to its wonder and delight,
not surrendering to its darkness
or its negative, trivial fight,
I journey free among the brilliant stars,
what they offer me that is so bright,
urging to see, longing to feel, craving to do what is good, or what is
real.
The majesty of the universe and nature abide in harmony since time
began,
I do not feed on the darkness, rather I bathe in the light, whenever I
can.

So whenever my heart has sunken so low that I can no longer see,
I reach for those stars that shine so bright paving my path for me.
They offer me hope, they offer me faith to keep on treading where I
must go,
they give me knowledge of who I am and the life I yearn to know.
So I shall always reach a litter higher for that one gleaming special
star,
I will for today, tell myself, that they really aren't all that far.
Give your dreams the opportunity of discovery and possibility to
come true,
never stop reaching for those stars, never stop reaching for something
new!

# Dorothy's Heart

A smile that is touched by heaven's grace,
A loving touch that brings
to hearts God's wondrous face,
A laugh that fills the
room with amazing delight,
A hug that consumes your
heart and gives you much more might,
to face what lies ahead
and gives you much more sight.
Sparkling eyes that beam
of tremendous affection,
they reflect deep inside of
you with incredible devotion.

Who could possess all these things wrapped up into one heart, one
soul?
I will tell you, if you feel
that you truly must know,
Her name was Dorothy,
an Aunt filled with so much care,
I can tell you, not once
was her heart ever bare.

The love, the guide of
my steps she gave to me,
she gave me wisdom and
taught me how to love, you see,
The one thing that will forever
live inside of my heart,
is the journey and travels of love, she gave to me from the very start.

I shall miss her, and my heart will always feel a gentle tug of grief,
but I shall see her again,
for our life here on earth,
in the over all scheme of things,
is really quite brief.

When you see someone love without conditions or judgments at all,
think of Aunt Dorothy's heart,
for that was truly her call.
I love you Aunt Dorothy!

*Cathy L. Kaiser*

# A Magical Journey

Imagination, Fantasy, Dreams and Reality,
all contained… all elements by one magical moment of belief.
One mystical reason of conception.

We draw reality, ideas, and reason,
we silently hope, dream, conceive,
imagine our dreams into existence.
All in one fleeting moment,
one splendid season.

If we posses what it takes to believe,
to surrender ourselves to the magic of sight,
bursting reality of magical light.
Embracing the beauty of the darkness
in the stillness of the night.

Knowing what we imagine can be,
Understanding what we dream, we can see,
Realizing what we fantasize, can be the key—

## To Our Own Reality

# America Unaware

Sleeping Beauty, America unaware,
land of riches, the land of the free,
a friend of other countries,
pounded by evil, not treated with any care.

Our eyes bound with a smoke of distress,
taken by the winds of darkest of souls,
giving us not a moment to feel at peace, to achieve any earned rest.
Waves of troubled waters roar in, our freedom at severe risk,
angry citizens pound with sorrow their fists.
our cries of the lost, souls of sorrow, even our comforts has taken
flight,
our light slammed to darkness,
our test is of our might.

Faceless cowards lurking
to give us no resolution,
Americans outraged running to revenge,
yet some yearning mere justice,
for what has to us been done,
what has seem to merely begun,
some hold their weapons high, as they sing of their foe's to die.
Some hold their faces in their hands and give themselves to a bellow,
a cry.

So then what is the true freedom song?
How can we right, what has been wrong?
Freedom, truth, justice and integrity, where now does it all belong?
given to a breathless wind, all put at risk, put to the ultimate test,
We must raise our flags high, with boldness hold up our heads with
great pride,
It is in truth, freedom and honor from which we are dressed.
It is Freedom, it is truth, it is America
that will be willing, that will with honor give her way to true justice,
that will grant to all what is best.

145

# Passage to your love

I take passage in the stillness of the night,
mindful and smiling on the good things that gently come to light.

What I see—

what I feel—

what is there, my love—is **YOU**.

You have embraced my fantasies.
You have quietly kissed my dreams.
Your drops of essence, so much alive, now runs in my veins.
In your soothing, sweet hands,
holds the treasures of my realities.

Oh my cherished love,
until the sun darkens,
until the moon glows no more,
until the stars loose their shine,
until time stands absolutely still,
and moves not at all,
until the infinite mountains crumble and fall.

You shall always be mine,
I will always belong to you,
our hearts standing invariably
so strong and true.

The promise of our love
existed before time began,
from the sun's first light,
our souls journeyed together—
surrendering to love's wondrous sight.

# The Last Mile Home

I gaze over the horizon, and I see
A beautiful red sunset with only a few
tired steps left for me.
Throughout my journey,
my spirit taken with anticipation
as I travel that last mile—
home—with determination.

Home—that very special territory
that is kept close to my inner core,
It is like no other-place, one of splendor,
one of mag—ic—one of glory!
Where beliefs and your dreams can soar high above the heavens,
Where the melody of your very spirit can be heard like never before.
Home—that wonder of
surroundings where your song can
truly give, where the tune of
your essence will forever live,
Where your spirit can freely sore!

Home—your refuge—your strength
—your corner stone,
a resting nest where you
are not ever truly alone.

Yes it is a place of wonder and delight,
where joys rises and laughter reigns!
A lodging of serenity, yes a place,
where there is no
longer a fight to fight.
Home—where creativity can truly come alive,
where reality and fantasies
can once again be revived.

*Cathy L. Kaiser*

That incredible abode where happiness and your heart always rules!
A place where true rapture of harmony abides,
Home—that residence of wonder, where stars you boldly ride!
Where you always succeed
and are the very best,
where unconditional love
takes care of all the rest.

Journey that last mile home.
Bathe in its majestic beauty,
let your essence hold that never ending, joyous smile,
as you travel toward home,
yes, that very last mile.

# Just For You

I have seen the waters rumble,
I have seen the stormy clouds gather,
I have felt the earth beneath me crumble,
I could hear the earth's crust chatter.

I have seen such mountains
that I not dare cross,
I have had such fear, I felt so lost.
I was consumed with such pain,
I couldn't go on,
I was given such heart ache,
I thought my very soul was gone.

Through it all, without a doubt, I can say this,
I was never, no, not for the slightest moment,
was I alone, but held gently in his hands,
For my foot he kept steady,
not one step did I miss,
He gave a peace that fell over me like a mist.

For when you think you battle all alone,
when you imagine, not one soul knows your passage, or your zone,
know that each step taken is in his very care,
that his heart is never empty,
no, for you it is never bare.

To watch your footing, to guide your ways,
To keep you safe, each of your days.
To know your heart, To give you more sight,
to show you His wonder,
to show you more of His light.

Not in a astonishing loud trumpet sound,
Not in shout or loud clouds
that thunders and roars,
but in a sweet moment, in one silent prayer,
that He has kept you, safe and aware.

In a whisper, in a gentle soft blowing wind,
He will guide you, and His
choir of angels he will send.
So know above all, that you are never just one,
That just for you,
He sent His only begotten Son.

# A Poet's Heart

Let the words fall from the very drops of your inner most spirit,
Let them be heard... let them speak...
Let go of your flesh that creates mortals to become so weak.

With fibers of your very heart,
painted with the words, whispers of the depths of the soul,
it was present from the beginning, a place—one since has never part.
Let the words greet the stars
and planets with a kiss,
it surrounds, the melody that gives wisdom,
for the words that offers the tune, that utters an incredible sound,
with such grace, such charm, the inner self can at last be found.

Hearts graced with the sweetest, surefire song,
imprinted on the glowing stars above,
comprehending all we savor, knowing without any doubts, we do
belong,
all part of the harmony as a whole, one small portion of the song,

Through the poet's heart we have uttered, we have lived, we have
touched,
We... from our inner eyes can truly see—
places and adventures that each and everyone
have at the very least, dreamed to be.

For when a poet paints such beauty, such blazing glory,
when that poet proclaims for humanity, their own private story,
it speaks for us all, it speaks to us all,
its speaks for you... it speaks for me... our very foundation does it
call.
Oh yes, a poet's heart indeed.

# A Timeless Glow

Endless passions, boundless imagination, ageless creativity,
beyond the mortal body, outside the city limits of spiritual realm.
A travel, a journey, a voyage,
an adventure to find,
all laid within the heart, within our very essence, our mind.

A Place where a cheerful heart embraces
each and every belief,
a place where once laid, sorrow and grief.

A place where there is no busy,
no appointments to keep,
a place for thought… none is too deep.

Where energies glow…
no recharge is needed,
a place where without restrictions,
with joy you dance!!
Where you can take without hesitation,
that very last chance.

Time expanded—this is so clear,
in the very depths, of my very heart—
there is no fear.
Time seemed to cease—
I was then given to release.

Now free from the flesh,
given to a radiant glow,
the rest, in your own time, in your own space,
you will learn, you shall without
one doubt, will know.

Give to your passion, surrender to its glow,
reach for the magic, never letting go.

# Reaching The Magic

Dream your dreams,
set your imagination free,
give to your creativity,
what it needs to be.

Reach for the magic,
believe it can be,
give to your vision,
let your inner eyes see.

Hold that star of hope,
believe with all you are,
reaching for what seems
to be a little bit too far.

Your faith can climb higher,
than any possibility.
Your dreams you can believe,
your fear you can relieve.

Dreams your dreams,
Yes, reach for the magic!

*Cathy L. Kaiser*

# Silence or sound?

A chair… a simple chair…
a chair bound with wheels,
the cries are silent that come
from those who sit there,
the sounds fall on deaf ears,
their hearts are compelled to share,
if only others could listen and
know where they are,
no one to assist the reaching
that seems so very far.
Doors shut in their faces,
ramps are too steep to climb,
windows slam on their hands,
As they try to reach as far as their bodies & hearts possibly can.

But who will listen to those who sit in a chair?
Their heads are bowed in great despair?
In the stores people run them over, bump into their chairs as if they do
not exist,
How they wish to shout, do I bump into your legs, or run you down??
It is difficult not to say,
not to come to a rage of anger,
it is most challenging to resist.
Deep within their essence forms a most discouraging frown,
if only deaf ears could hear their cries,
their sounds.

Who will open their ears and let the emotions run to their very hearts?
Who will hear the cries of the person who needs the sounds
of their voice not to merely depart?
Who will hear the voice in the chair,
bound with wheels,
who will listen to that voice
in a prison of such silence?

Who will take hold of the hand of the broken body and heart?
I wonder… just who will merely take a moment and listen to their
voice,
what is your choice?
Silence or sound?

# The Journey Home

My heart is full, my spirit in awe,
God's amazing grace bestowed to each one, yes to us all.
Reflecting over each year, looking back over all the laughter we
shared,
reflecting the joy we held, remembering each fear and every tear.
Understanding so many things we had so deeply cared.

Comprehending that life goes beyond infinity,
through the shimmering stars, the thriving planets, and the glowing
moon,
right past the heavens'
golden gates all too very soon.
Through our earthly years
we are merely a guest,
as we walk our passage, we do our best,
to show our inner light
from the depths of our soul,
to give... to love... to with truth sojourn
honoring our lives with
our goodness and what we know.

To be willing to share and show love in a selfless manner,
giving ourselves unconditionally,
believing it does not matter.
To smile with our hearts,
to give with our hands,
to laugh and wiggle our toes in the sand.

To not allow "the busy" sickness take us by the rapid storm's wind,
to always make time for another, to have a hand to lend.
For in the scheme of all things, for the bigger purpose we know,
that holding love close to our hearts and time to let it show,
will bring our lives to a place to rejoice, to flourish and grow,

It will cause a melody from our depths to be heard from the sky,
it will create our very heart's
existence and it will not ever die..
So take the time to share your heart,
give all you possibly can,
in the silence of your inner
essence take that honorable stand.
For our journey is not far from home, only a mile or two left to
pursue,
take that pathway home
those who travel it are but a few.

Give the stars above your
song to burst out and ring,
By each word or deed, give life to your music,
give voice to your song to sing.
Until then, my friend, let us continue in harmony this journey home.
One or two miles on our path, traveling towards the light,
making our way through
the darkness of the night.
Yes, our journey home.

# Our Inner Voice

Hearts tumbling,
inner voice rumbling,
so many voices urging to speak,
nothing inside left to be meek.

Bones crushing,
emotions rushing,
flowing like a fountain,
meeting heights of the highest mountain.

Echoes so distant,
whispers quietly given from long ago,
aiding to what we all ready know.

Step after step we cautiously take,
answers to questions we urgently make.
Our destination held like a treasure,
with every single adventure,
we carefully consider each
and every measure.

A mere mile or two left to travel,
trusting that our hearts will not unravel.
Holding on to each peaceful thought,
that all will be attained that we so
diligently sought.

# Inward Sight

Kisses of Time,
Echoes of the past,
Whispers of hope for the future,
All within one breath,
One soft heart beat, one speechless prayer.

It is but a transient moment,
that I hold this cherished treasure
so tenderly, so dear,
it vanishes with the wind,
before there is time to fear.

Feeling each warm smile,
touching each shed tear,
embracing all things year after year,
it points the way to who I am,
to who I am destined to be.
Causing the fibers of my
heart and eyes, to truly see.

# Faces

So many faces we try on for a fit,
some brings others closer to our heart,
we know, that it isn't quite it.

Some we try on in the morning light,
Some, in the midst of the dawn,
Some we show, as we stand in our lawn.
some sing a tune, during the dimmest night.
Yet, all in all, it always works out just right.

Faces of wonder,
faces of delight,
faces of strength to aid my fight.

Faces of mercy,
sight when I am blind & lost,
faces of knowing the honest worth
of the humility of cost.

Faces of freedom,
true faces of honor,
in all sincerity, what our hearts conceive,
and in all that we truly believe.

Hearts delighted,
all the heavens rejoiced,
Yes, the angels' choirs give way to their voice!
I realize that each and every day,
that I in fact have a choice!

So many faces we wear,
for our hearts are so full of care.
So many faces do we enhance,
as our smiles come to our lips,
we give away to that special, joyous dance!

What faces do you wear?

# The Silent Cry

The earth weeps in awed silence,
for all we have stolen, for all it has lost,
because we have taken without giving,
for others will pay a tremendous cost.

We live as if there is no tomorrow,
"drink! and be merry we say,"
what happens to our great grandchildren,
when no more food the
earth can bring their way?

What happens when the earth
can no longer be tilled,
what happens, when she
loses her very own will?
Oh yes what happens when
she grows of tired of giving,
and time stands still for the living?
What happens with darkness
creeps over her face,
and no longer is there light within her grace.

Who will cry for her in silence then?

# The Wings Of The Morning

The breaking of the morning clouds,
to see the sun bring forth its light,
to see the untold strength
and practiced courage,
To feel the amazing might!

The boundless compassion with a giving heart and a sound mind,
Things become endless of what
on this journey for me might shine.
Life's lessons set before me,
with choices in each hand,
one decision, one inner smile,
from making that strategic stand,
on choices towards home, one more mile.

My thoughts that are blessed by angels,
they are more than the number of the sand,
when I sleep or am awake,
they remain with me,
it springs the magic of belief and aids my inner sight to truly see.
It gives to me, a peace that
is beyond the mention of words,
An unspeakable joy springs from my very soul,
Yes these things without
a glimmer of doubt, do I know.

For I am persuaded that neither death nor life,
nor angels, nor powers of any kind,
that even in the face of things present,
or things to come,
nor what life brings for me to find.

I am convinced that no
matter what height or depth,
no matter what creature has been kept,
that this love, this very love our
creator gives so freely as a gift,
will always surround me and
give my very essence a lift.

For if I take the wings of the morning and dwell
in the uttermost parts of the earth or sea,
even there shall His very hand
know just where to lead me,
to each path I should tread,
And to every adventure I shall go, to each and every tear I shed.
All these things, I have mindfully said.

To every bit of laughter of sound,
Yes in every single place, His love I have always found.
His strength, His courage shall give my eyes the direction I am bound.

To endure each passage that may be somewhat rough,
He gives that depth of inner power just when my way gets too tough.
He delights when I find my heart, and just who I was intended to be,

His laughter of joy do I hear, when I have the courage to listen and
just be me!

Yes the wings of the morning,
that breaks the dark sky,
the wings of the morning, I could never deny.

# Four Faces Of Passion

Four faces of passion,
blended parts of the whole,
single elements to reach the ultimate goal.

Anger—Joy—Laughter—& Grief,
each to their own, each can be so brief.

Four faces of passion all rolled into one,
giving way to every need,
when its work is finally done.
Truth unbridled, such inner sight.
I mindfully take the wings
for my adventurous flight.
Radiant hope, untold imagination soars, cherished dreams of magic,
a refuge from what could be ever so tragic.

Tears of fire, secretly wept,
holding, embracing all that I kept.
Laughter ignites my heart ablaze,
giving my most inner spirit an inspiring raise!!

Oh yes, the four faces of passion, I cannot lie,
a piece of the puzzle I will not deny.
Each part of the whole is needed you see,
for it takes each and every part, to set me free,
Yes, it takes each part, to let me be me!

# One Love, One Life

Tears trickle down the soul filled with
so much passion. So much love,
so much that it cannot be kept still.
So much inside that what rushes in my soul
are enormous thrills.

Arms aching to hold—Heart shaking to love
Soul shivering to embrace.

**Only one soul** can give me all that I need,

**Only one soul** do I wish to love and love indeed!

**Only one soul** can I give, all that I have to share.

**Only one soul** do all of me wish to bare.

**Only one soul** in my love can truly live.

Laughter rings, Essence sings,
body of passion shivers
When you are near, with you there are no fears.

Love felt so strong, knowing we belong,
to end each day
in each others arms drifting to
that sweet peaceful place
our place of dreams. Before drifting there,
to caress your sweet face.
Oh my sweet angel, I dream only of you.

# The Cocoon

Releasing to the endless stars things of old, things long past.
Embracing those things that will surely last.
Comprehending death as not an end,
rather a true glorious beginning.
Measuring how much love my heart can send.


Not as a flower that withers away,
not by mere words as some would say.
By the heart, each action, every deed,
as if I was watching a plant grow from the tiniest seed.


A caterpillar weaves its own web of death,
yes its own, dark, snug cocoon,
but definitely alone.


He awaits for that one moment
of glory for us to be shown.
For that one special moment of truth
when his beauty can unfold,
his wings spread in splendor
and ride the wind to see his new world,
or this is what have been for ages told.

He welcomes freedom to become his own,
and finally flourish from
the seed that he had sown.
Without his dark cocoon
he would have been lost,
for every enchantment, there is a cost.

So let the morning light shine bright,
that it will enlighten our depths of inner sight.


Yes my friend, Death is but a mere beginning.

# Love That Never Dies

We had been together for years, here it was early for Sunday morning, she was busy reading her morning paper. I gazed at her, thinking how much time had passed, how I should feel just comfortable and a bit bored with her by this time. She lifted her coffee cup and sipped on her coffee like every morning, it caused a smile to break out on my lips.

I thought, my here we are still together and in my heart a torch burned with a blazing fire for her, oh yes much more than the day before. How is that possible? After all this time, day after day, month after month, year after year—I was not bored with her, I still found her enticing, exciting, and the love that existed between us was still more than astonishing.

She glanced up and looked at me, giggled and said, "What is it?" I gave her a half-grin and said, "oh I just think we have a pretty pleasant life." She smiled. In her eyes I could see all the possibilities, no limitations, no boundaries. In the mirror of her soul, I could see that I could do anything, no matter the odds against me. In her eyes I could see total freedom from all the limits I impose upon myself that prevented me from accomplishing what I need to do, what I most desire to do. In her eyes, was magic, yes indeed magic of possibilities! Magic of Hope!! Magic of belief! In her eyes, I could see my whole world there.

Her belief in me set my most inner spirit free, those drops of essence that allow me to know who I am. Yes, such freedom contained in her eyes, as if the binding chains that kept me prisoner, just fell from me like petals from a blooming rose. She creates an unquenchable thirst for life, for love, for all good things.

She causes the bountiful desire to search for the roads not taken, to celebrate every moment of living as if it was my last moment to know, to see, to feel. She brings about a laughter deep inside of me to break out in song, for happiness to ring out until the stars lose their sparkle, their very light.

What I know, what I feel for her is timeless, it is an undying love that has left prints upon the stars, it is as endless as the vast sky above. It will continue on as long as time exists, as long as people willingly love each other and reach out to one another with their hearts full of purity, honesty, and the desire to give. Our never-ending love for each other shall remain as a glowing beacon, to give passage to many others throughout many worlds to come.

I smiled, picked up my cup of tea, and took a drink and set it back down, looked up at her and said, "so dear, what is the agenda for the day?"

# About the Author

I was born in 1956 in the Midwest, one of six children, growing up in a Christian environment. In 1998, we moved to Phoenix, Arizona. I am a lover of nature, music and the arts. The household consists of me, my companion Laura, and two four-legged family members, Mariah and Jazz. Some of the obstacles I've overcome, five back surgeries resulting in partial disability, causing many challenges, and many years of recovering from drug addiction. My poetry is about these challenges and the celebrations that come from them.

The journey is written, but the destiny not yet set.